McGraw-Hill's
# Super-Mini
# American Slang
## Dictionary

# McGraw-Hill's
# *Super-Mini*
# *American Slang*
# Dictionary

## Second Edition

### Richard A. Spears, Ph.D.

New York  Chicago  San Francisco  Lisbon  London  Madrid  Mexico City
Milan  New Delhi  San Juan  Seoul  Singapore  Sydney  Toronto

**Library of Congress Cataloging-in-Publication Data**

Spears, Richard A.
   McGraw-Hill's super-mini American slang dictionary / Richard A. Spears. — [2nd. ed.].
      p.   cm. — (McGraw-Hill Super mini)
   Previous ed.: NTC's super-mini American slang dictionary. 1st ed. Lincolnwood, Ill.,
USA : National Textbook Co., ©1996.
   ISBN 0-07-149228-3 (alk. paper)
   1. English language—United States—Slang—Dictionaries.   2. Americanisms—
Dictionaries.   I. Spears, Richard A. Contemporary American slang.   II. Title.
III. Title: Super-mini American slang dictionary.   IV. Title: American slang dictionary.

PE2846.S65   2007
427'.97303—dc22

2007016944

1 2 3 4 5 6 7 8 9 10 11 12 13 14 15 16 17 18 19 20   TRA/TRA   0 9 8 7

ISBN-13: 978-0-07-149228-7
ISBN-10:    0-07-149228-3

Illustrations by Luc Nisset
Interior design by Terry Stone

McGraw-Hill books are available at special quantity discounts to use as premiums and sales
promotions, or for use in corporate training programs. For more information, please write to
the Director of Special Sales, Professional Publishing, McGraw-Hill, Two Penn Plaza, New
York, NY 10121-2298. Or contact your local bookstore.

**Also in this series:**

*McGraw-Hill's Super-Mini American Idioms Dictionary*
*McGraw-Hill's Super-Mini Phrasal Verb Dictionary*

# Contents

# Introduction to the
# Second Edition

This dictionary is a resource cataloging the meaning and usage of frequently occurring slang and colloquial expressions in the U.S.A. It contains expressions that are familiar to many Americans and other expressions that are used primarily within small groups of people. These expressions come from movies, novels, newspaper stories, and everyday conversation. The entries represent the vocabulary found in many places, such as the college campus and urban streets. We hear slang from surfers, weight lifters, and young people in general.

There is no standard test that will decide what is slang and what is not. Expressions that are identified as slang are sometimes little more than entertaining wordplay, and much slang is little more than an entertaining, alternative way of saying something. Slang is rarely the first choice of careful writers or speakers or anyone attempting to use language for formal, persuasive, or business purposes. Nonetheless, expressions that can be called slang make up a major part of American communication in movies, television, radio, newspapers, magazines, and informal spoken conversation.

Young people are responsible for a high proportion of the fad expressions and collegiate wordplay found here. It is no surprise that there are a large number of clever expressions for sex, drinking, and vomiting from this source. Other matters of social taboo have provided many slang expressions as well. Although, strictly speaking, taboo words are not slang, the major taboo words have been included in this dictionary.

Many of us enjoy "presenting" a new slang term to a listener by slipping it into conversation. As listeners, many of us enjoy hearing a new slang term and figuring out what it means, using context, setting, and our own brain power. This element of social wordplay is primarily what attracts word-wise people to slang and what makes a dictionary of this type interesting reading as well as a useful reference work.

This edition is a 2,000-entry abridgement of the fourth edition of *McGraw-Hill's American Slang Dictionary* and focuses on recent slang as well as a selection of entertaining locutions that exhibit the highly creative nature of slang and its users.

# Terms, Symbols, and Abbreviations

◆ marks the beginning of an example in the main dictionary and serves as a separator in the indexes.

[ ] enclose parts of a definition that aid in its understanding but are not represented in the entry head.

**abb.** abbreviation, referring to both acronyms and initialisms.

**acronym** a kind of abbreviation where the initial letters or syllables of the words of a phrase are combined into a pronounceable word, such as GIGO = garbage in, garbage out.

**AND** indicates that additional variants follow.

**black** people of African descent and other dark-skinned people.

**cliché** an overly familiar and trite phrase.

**comp. abb.** computer abbreviation, the initialisms and acronyms used in computer communications, such as email and instant messaging.

**exclam.** an exclamation.

**Go to** indicates that the information you want is at the entry listed after **Go to**. Leave this entry and go to the one indicated.

**in.** an intransitive verb or phrase containing an intransitive verb.

**initialism** a kind of abbreviation where the initial letters of the words in a phrase are pronounced one by one, such as BCNU = Be seein' you.

**interj.** an interjection.

**interrog.** an interrogative.

**mod.** a modifier of some type, such as an adjective or adverb.

**n.** noun or noun phrase.

**phr.** a phrase.

**pro.** a pronoun.

**See also** indicates that there is additional information at the entry listed after **See also**. Consult or consider the entry indicated. It is not required that you visit the indicated entry to understand the current entry. **See also** does not mean "synonymous with" the entry indicated.

**sent.** a sentence.

**so** someone.

**sth** something.

**streets** slang associated with street gangs and the popular "gangsta" culture. Many elements are taken from the rap or hip-hop music scene.

**taboo** avoided in polite, formal, dignified, older, or refined settings.

**term of address** a word that can be used to address a person directly.

**tv.** a transitive verb or phrase containing a transitive verb.

**underworld** slang from criminal and organized crime. Overlaps with **streets**.

**white** people of European descent and other light-skinned people.

# Pronunciation Guide

Some expressions in the dictionary are followed by a phonetic transcription in International Phonetic Alphabet (IPA) symbols. These expressions include words whose pronunciations are not predictable from their spellings, difficult or unfamiliar words, and words where the stress placement is contrastive or unique. The style of pronunciation reflected here is informal and tends to fit the register in which the expression would normally be used. A [d] is used for the alveolar flap typical in American pronunciations such as [wɑdɚ] "water" and [əˈnɑɪələdəd] "annihilated." The transcriptions distinguish between [ɑ] and [ɔ] and between [w] and [ʍ] even though not all Americans do so. In strict IPA fashion, [j] rather than the [y] substitute is used for the initial sound in "yellow." The most prominent syllable in a multisyllabic word is preceded by a [ˈ]. The use of "and" or "or" in a phonetic transcription echoes the use of "and" or "or" in the preceding entry phrase. The use of "..." in a transcription indicates that easy-to-pronounce words have been omitted. Parentheses used in a transcription either correspond to parentheses in the preceding entry phrase or indicate optional elements in the transcription. For instance, in [ˈɑrtsi ˈkræf(t)si] "artsy-craftsy," the "t" may or may not be pronounced. The following chart shows the American English values for each of the IPA symbols used in the phonetic transcriptions. To use the chart, first find the large phonetic symbol whose value you want to determine. The two English words to the right of the symbol contain examples of the sound for which the phonetic symbol stands. The letters in **boldface** type indicate where the sound in question is found in the English word.

| | | | | | | | |
|---|---|---|---|---|---|---|---|
| [ɑ] | st**o**p<br>t**o**p | [ɚ] | b**ir**d<br>t**ur**tle | [n] | **n**ew<br>fu**nn**y | [tʃ] | **ch**eese<br>pit**ch**er |
| [æ] | s**a**t<br>tr**a**ck | [f] | **f**eel<br>i**f** | [ŋ] | butto**n**<br>kitte**n** | [θ] | **th**in<br>fai**th** |
| [ɑu] | c**ow**<br>n**ow** | [g] | **g**et<br>fro**g** | [ŋ] | bri**ng**<br>thi**ng** | [u] | f**oo**d<br>bl**ue** |
| [ɑɪ] | b**i**te<br>m**y** | [h] | **h**at<br>**wh**o | [o] | c**oa**t<br>wr**o**te | [ʊ] | p**u**t<br>l**oo**k |
| [b] | **b**eet<br>**b**u**bb**le | [i] | f**ee**l<br>l**ea**k | [ɔɪ] | sp**oi**l<br>b**oy** | [v] | sa**v**e<br>**v**an |
| [d] | **d**ead<br>bo**d**y | [ɪ] | b**i**t<br>h**i**ss | [ɔ] | c**au**ght<br>**yaw**n | [w] | **w**ell<br>**w**ind |
| [ð] | **th**at<br>**th**ose | [j] | **y**ellow<br>**y**ou | [p] | **t**i**p**<br>**p**at | [ʍ] | **wh**eel<br>**wh**ile |
| [dʒ] | **j**ail<br>**j**u**dg**e | [k] | **c**an<br>**k**eep | [r] | **r**at<br>be**rr**y | [z] | fu**zz**y<br>**z**oo |
| [e] | d**a**te<br>s**ai**l | [l] | **l**awn<br>yel**l**ow | [s] | **s**un<br>fa**s**t | [ʒ] | plea**s**ure<br>trea**s**ure |
| [ɛ] | g**e**t<br>s**e**t | [ɬ] | bott**le**<br>pudd**le** | [ʃ] | **f**i**sh**<br>**s**ure | ['] | '**water**<br>ho'**tel** |
| [ə] | b**u**t<br>n**u**t | [m] | fa**m**ily<br>sla**m** | [t] | **t**op<br>po**t** | | |

# A

**abbreviated piece of nothing** *n.* an insignificant person or thing. ♦ *Tell that abbreviated piece of nothing to get his tail over here, but fast.*

**abe** *n.* a five-dollar bill. (From the picture of Abraham Lincoln on the bill.) ♦ *This wine cost three abes. It had better be good.*

**abolic** *n.* anabolic steroids as used by veterinarians and abused by humans. ♦ *You keep taking in that abolic, and you'll swell up and die!*

**abs** [æbz] *n.* the abdominal muscles. (Bodybuilding. See also **washboard abs**.) ♦ *Look at the abs on that guy. Like a crossword puzzle!*

**action 1.** *n.* excitement; activity in general; whatever is happening. ♦ *This place is dull. I want some action!* **2.** *n.* a share of something; a share of the winnings or of the booty. ♦ *I did my share of the work, and I want my share of the action.* **3.** *n.* sex; copulation. ♦ *All those guys are just trying for a little action.* **4.** *n.* illegal activity; commerce in drugs; acts of crime. (Underworld.) ♦ *Things have been a little slow here, but there's some action on the East Coast.*

**Adam Henry** *n.* an AH = **asshole**, = **jerk**. Treated as a name. ♦ *Why don't you get some smarts, Adam Henry?*

**addy** *n.* address. ♦ *What's your addy so I can send you an invitation?*

**AFAIK** *phr.* as far as I know. (Acronym. Computers and the Internet.) ♦ *Everything is okay with the server, AFAIK.*

**ag** AND **aggro** *mod.* aggrivated = irritated: annoyed. ♦ *Hey, man. Don't get yourself so aggro!* ♦ *She said she was too "ag" to help with the dishes.*

**AH** *n.* an asshole; a really wretched person. (A euphemistic disguise. Also a term of address. Rude and derogatory.) ♦ *Look here, you goddamn AH! Who the hell do you think you are?*

**aight** *mod.* all right. (Streets.) ♦ *Aight, my bruva, aight, aight.*

**ain't long enough** *phr.* of a sum of money that isn't adequate; without adequate funds. (Streets.) ♦ *I can't go with you. I ain't long enough.*

**air biscuit** *n.* a breaking of wind; a fart. ♦ *Who is responsible for that air biscuit?*

**air guitar** *n.* an imaginary guitar, played along with real music. ♦ *Jed, who sees himself as some sort of rock star, plays air guitar when he's happy or sad.*

**air hose** *n.* invisible socks; no socks. ♦ *How do you like my new air hose? One size fits all.*

**air kiss** *n.* a kiss that is placed on the inside of the fingers of one's hand then "blown" to the recipient who is likely to be some distance away. ♦ *A mass of air kisses drifted down to the wharf from the passengers departing on the huge Titanic.*

air guitar

**airish** *mod.* [of the weather] chilly or briskly cool. ♦ *It's airish enough to freeze the brass off a bald monkey!*

**All options stink.** AND **AOS** *phr. & comp. abb.* All options stink.; There is no good solution. ♦ *I don't know what to do. All options stink.* ♦ *Since AOS, I'll do nothing at all.*

**all sharped up** *mod.* dressed up; looking sharp. ♦ *Chuckie, my man, you are totally sharped up.*

**all show and no go** *phr.* equipped with good looks but lacking action or energy. (Used to describe someone or something that looks good but does not perform as promised.) ♦ *That shiny car of Jim's is all show and no go.*

**all-nighter 1.** *n.* something that lasts all night, like a party or study session. ♦ *After an all-nighter studying, I couldn't keep my eyes open for the test.* **2.** *n.* a place of business that is open all night. ♦ *We stopped at an all-nighter for a cup of coffee.* **3.** *n.* a person who often stays up all night. ♦ *I'm no all-nighter. I need my beauty sleep, for sure.*

**Am I right?** *interrog.* Isn't that so?; Right? (A way of demanding a response and stimulating further conversation.) ♦ *You want to make something of yourself. Am I right?*

**ammo** ['æmo] **1.** *n.* ammunition. ♦ *There they were, trapped in a foxhole with no ammo, enemy all over the place. What do you think happened?* **2.** *n.* information or evidence that can be used to support an argument or a charge. ♦ *I want to get some ammo on the mayor. I think he's a crook.*

**ammunition 1.** *n.* toilet tissue. ♦ *Could somebody help me? We're out of ammunition in here!* **2.** *n.* liquor. ♦ *He's had about all the ammunition he can hold.*

**anal applause** *n.* the release of intestinal gas. (Jocular.) ♦ *Who is responsible for this pungent anal applause?*

**and a half** *n.* someone or something greater, more severe, or more intense than normal. ♦ *This computer problem is a mess and a half!*

**angle 1.** *n.* a person's understanding of something; someone's unique perspective on an event or happening. ♦ *What Bob says is interesting. What's your angle on this, Molly?* **2.** *n.* a scheme or deception; a pivotal or critical feature of a scheme; the gimmick in a scheme or plot. ♦ *I got a new angle to use in a con job on the old guy.*

**ante** [ænti] **1.** *n.* an amount of money that must be contributed before playing certain card games such as poker. ♦ *That's a pretty high ante. Forget it!* **2.** *n.* the charge or cost. ♦ *What's the ante for a used 1985 four-door?*

**antsy** ['æntsi] *mod.* nervous; restless. ♦ *She gets antsy before a test.*

**aped** [ept] *mod.* alcohol intoxicated. ♦ *I've never seen my brother so totally aped before.*

**apeshit 1.** *mod.* excited; freaked out. <@t-italic> *He was so apeshit about that dame!* **2.** *mod.* drunk. (Acting as strangely or comically as an ape.) ♦ *The guy was really apeshit. Couldn't even stand up.*

**app** *n.* an application; a computer software application. ♦ *Ted's killer app can run circles around your old Word-Sun program.*

**apples to oranges** AND **A2O** *phr. & comp. abb.* [but that's comparing] apples to oranges; [You are] making an unfair comparison. ♦ *Chevvies and Beemers! That's apples to oranges! They're not even in the same class!* ♦ *It's A2O! What can I say?*

**arb** [ɑrb] *n.* an arbitrageur; a market speculator. (Securities markets.) ♦ *I wanted to be an arb, but it takes about forty million to get in the door.*

**Are we having fun yet?** AND **AWHFY** *sent. & comp. abb.* This isn't the fun that you stated or implied it would be, is it? ♦ *Are we having fun yet? This is really dull.* ♦ *Gr8t! AWHFY?*

**areous** *n.* [an] area. (Streets.) ♦ *Keep that baby gangsta outa ma areous!*

**ark** [ɑrk] *n.* an old car. ♦ *Why don't you get rid of that old ark and get something that's easier to park?*

**artillery 1.** *n.* handguns; grenades. (Underworld.) ♦ *Where does Frank stash the artillery?* **2.** *n.* flatware; cutlery. ♦ *Who put out the artillery? I didn't get a fork.*

**as a matter of fact** AND **AAMOF** *phr. & comp. abb.* actually; in fact. ♦ *AAMOF, Bob just came in.* ♦ *As a matter of fact, he's right here. You want to talk to him?*

**(as) close as stink on shit** *phr.* very close; intimate; inseparable. ♦ *In love? He's as close to her as stink on shit.*

**(as) fat as a beached whale** *phr.* very, very fat. ♦ *That dame is as fat as a beached whale.*

**As if!** AND **AI** *exclam.* an expression said when someone says something that is not true but wishes that it were. (Also, and perhaps usually, sarcastic.) ♦ *A: I've got a whole lot of good qualities. B: AI!* ♦ *My hair should look like a pile of wet thatch? As if!*

**As if I care!** AND **AIIC** *exclam. & comp. abb.* What has led you to believe that I care at all? (See also **As if!**) ♦ *So he left you. AIIC!* ♦ *So, some hairdresser jerk dyed your hair orange! As if I care!*

**ass over tit** *mod.* [of someone falling] rolling and bounding over. (Usually objectionable.) ♦ *He fell, ass over tit, down the stairs.*

**asshat 1.** *n.* the imaginary garment worn by one with one's head up one's ass. (Offensive.) **2.** *n.* a person said to be wearing an **asshat** (sense 1). ♦ *Wake up, you stupid asshat!*

**at a snail's pace** AND **at a snail's gallop** *mod.* very slowly. ♦ *Poor old Willy is creeping at a snail's gallop* because his car has a flat tire. ♦ *The building project is coming along at a snail's pace.*

**ate up with** so/sth *mod.* consumed with someone or something; intrigued by someone or something. ♦ *Bob is really ate up with his new girlfriend.*

**attic** *n.* the head, thought of as the location of one's intellect. ♦ *She's just got nothing in the attic. That's what's wrong with her.*

**awesome 1.** *exclam.* Great!; Excellent! (Usually **Awesome!** Standard English, but used often in slang.) ♦ *You own that gorgeous hog? Awesome!* **2.** *mod.* impressive. ♦ *That thing is so awesome!*

**AWHFY** Go to Are we having fun yet?

**AWOL** [e 'dəblju 'o 'ɛl OR 'ewɑl] *mod.* absent without leave; escaped from prison or from the military. (Acronym or initialism.) ♦ *If I don't get back to the base, they're going to think I'm AWOL.*

**axe** *n.* a musical instrument. (Originally a saxophone.) ♦ *Get out your axe and let's jam.*

# B

**B. and B.** *mod.* breast and buttock, having to do with entertainment featuring female nudity. ♦ *Many movies add a little B. and B. just to get an R-rating.*

**babe 1.** AND **babes** *n.* a term of endearment for a woman or a man. (Also a term of address. See also **baby**.) ♦ *Look, babe, get in there and tackle that guy! We're losing!* ♦ *Hey, babes, let's us two get this done and head on home.* **2.** *n.* a good-looking woman. ♦ *Who is that babe standing on the corner over there?* ♦ *I saw you with that orange-haired babe last night. What's the story?*

**babe magnet** AND **chick magnet 1.** *n.* a male who seems to attract good looking females easily. ♦ *Keep your woman away from Chuck. He's a babe magnet.* ♦ *Wilfred thinks he's a chick magnet, but he only snags the dogs.* **2.** *n.* something, such as a car, that attracts good-looking females to a male. ♦ *Man, I like your new chick magnet. Get any yet?* ♦ *He thought of a new car as a "babe magnet," but all it drew was the repo man.*

**baby gangsta** AND **BG** *n.* a baby gangster; a fake gangster. (Streets.) ♦ *He's just a baby gangsta. Got a lot of growing to do.* ♦ *Little "BGs" grow up to be real ones.*

**babycakes** AND **honeycakes** *n.* a term of endearment; sweetie; dear. (Also a term of address.) ♦ *Look, honey-*

bad hair day

*cakes, I found some lipstick on your collar. ♦ Gee, baby-cakes, it must be yours!*

**back up** *in.* to refuse to go through with something; to back out (of something). ♦ *Fred backed up at the last minute, leaving me with twenty pounds of hot dogs.*

**backed up** *mod.* drug intoxicated. ♦ *Old Benny's really backed up.*

**backfire** *in.* to release intestinal gas anally and audibly. (Usually objectionable.) ♦ *Whew! Somebody backfired!*

**backhander** *n.* a backhand slap in the face. ♦ *Yes, officer, a perfectly strange woman came up and clobbered me with a backhander that loosened a tooth.*

**bad hair day** *n.* a bad day in general. (Also used literally when one's inability to do anything with one's hair seems to color the events of the day.) ♦ *I'm sorry I am so glum. This has been a real bad hair day.*

**bad paper** *n.* bad checks; a bad check. ♦ *She got six months for passing bad paper.*

**baddy** AND **baddie** ['bædi] *n.* a bad thing or person. ♦ *Using butter is supposed to be a real "baddy."* ♦ *Don't be such a baddie. Tell me you just love my hair!*

**bag on** SO **1.** *in.* to criticize someone. ♦ *Stop bagging on me! I'm tired of all your complaining.* **2.** *n.* to tease someone. ♦ *He is always bagging on his little sister.*

**Bag that!** *tv.* Forget that! ♦ *There are four—no, bag that!—six red ones and three blue ones.*

**Bag your face!** *exclam.* Go away! ♦ *You are so in the way! Bag your face!*

**bail on** SO *in.* to walk out on someone; to leave someone. ♦ *She bailed on me after all we had been through together.*

**bake the tube steak** *tv.* to copulate. ♦ *Bobby was set to bake the tube steak last night, but he failed to preheat the oven.*

**baldwin** *n.* a good-looking male. (As in Alec Baldwin.) ♦ *Who is that Baldwin I saw you with last night?*

**The ball is in** SO's **court.** *phr.* to be someone else's move, play, or turn. ♦ *I can't do anything as long as the ball is in John's court.*

**ball-breaker** AND **ball-buster 1.** *n.* a difficult task; a difficult or trying situation requiring extremely hard work or effort. (Usually objectionable.) ♦ *That whole construction job was a real ball-breaker.* ♦ *Why should moving furniture end up being such a ball-buster?* **2.** *n.* a hard taskmaster; a hard-to-please boss. (Usually objectionable.) ♦ *Tom gets a day's work for a day's pay out of his men, but he's no ball-breaker.* ♦ *My boss is a ball-buster, but he pays well.* **3.** *n.* a female who is threatening to males. (Usually objectionable.) ♦ *Mrs. Samuels has a terrible reputation as a "ball-breaker." Wholly deserved, I might add.*

**baller** *n.* an athlete. (One who plays with footballs, basketballs, baseballs, etc.) ♦ *You will make a lot of money as a professional baller.*

**ballhead** *n.* an athlete; someone obsessed with ball games. (Perhaps a stupid one.) ♦ *If you want to be a ballhead, you have to have talent and stamina.*

**balloon knot** *n.* the anus (From its appearance.) ♦ *Yeeeouch! Right in the balloon knot!*

**balloons** *n.* a woman's breasts, especially large ones. (Usually objectionable.) ♦ *What fine balloons on Jim's girl!*

**baloney pony** *n.* the penis. (Contrived for the sake of the rhyme.) ♦ *All he could think about was riding the old baloney pony.*

**baltic** *mod.* cold; very cold. ♦ *It really looks baltic out there today.*

**bam and scram** *n.* a hit and run accident. ♦ *The sirens were blaring and a dozen black and white headed to a bam and scram over on Maple.*

**bamma** *n.* a rural person, such as someone from Alabama; a hick. (Rude and derogatory.) ♦ *Some bamma in a pickup truck nearly ran me off the road.*

**banana-head** *n.* a stupid person. (Usually objectionable.) ♦ *Ask that banana-head why she is wearing a coat like that in July.*

**bang for the buck** *n.* value for the money spent; excitement for the money spent; the cost-to-benefit ratio. ♦ *How much bang for the buck did you really think you would get from a twelve-year-old car—at any price?*

**bang in (sick)** *in.* to call in sick. ♦ *Two more people just banged in sick!*

**banger 1.** *n.* the front bumper of a vehicle. ♦ *Other than a dent or two in the banger, this buggy's okay.* **2.** *n.* a hypodermic syringe. (Drugs.) ♦ *Jed dropped his banger and really panicked when it broke.*

**banging 1.** *mod.* good; exciting. ♦ *We had a banging good time at the concert.* **2.** *mod.* good looking; attractive. ♦ *Who was that banging chick I saw you with last night?* **3.** *mod.* [of music] loud. ♦ *That band is really banging. I think I am deaf!*

**bareback** *mod.* [copulating] without a condom. ♦ *I couldn't find a raincoat, and she wouldn't let me do it bareback.*

**barking spider** AND **trumpet spider** *n.* the imaginary source of the sound of an audible release of intestinal gas. (With reference to the image of an anus.) ♦ *Heidi, do you know anything about the trumpet spider I keep hearing?* ♦ *Although Dr. Waddlington-Stowe had never heard "barking spider" with reference to the affected part, he caught the connection immediately.*

**Barney 1.** *n.* the penis, especially if erect. (Usually a nickname. Alludes to color.) ♦ *Now, put Barney away and* *let's talk about our relationship.* **2.** *n.* a **nerd**; a **wimp**; an unattractive male. (From the Flintstones character or the children's dinosaur character.) ♦ *If you weren't such a Barney, you'd stick up for your own rights.* **3.** *n.* a good-looking guy. ♦ *Man she's really found herself a Barney!*

**barracuda** *n.* a predatory person, especially a predatory woman. ♦ *She's a barracuda. Better watch out!*

**base** *mod.* rude; gross. (California.) ♦ *You are so, like, base!*

**bashed** [bæʃt] **1.** *mod.* crushed; struck. ♦ *Give me that bashed one, and I'll straighten it out.* **2.** *mod.* alcohol intoxicated. ♦ *All four of them went out and got bashed.*

**bathtub scum** *n.* a totally despised person. (Also a term of address.) ♦ *Look out, bathtub scum, outa my way!*

**battle of the bulge** *n.* the attempt to keep one's waistline normal. (Named for a World War II battle.) ♦ *She appears to have lost the battle of the bulge.*

**bazillion** [bəˈzɪljən] *n.* an indefinite, enormous number. ♦ *Ernie gave me a bazillion good reasons why he shouldn't do it.*

**bazoom(s)** *n.* a woman's breasts; the female bosom. (Usually objectionable.) ♦ *I don't know how it happened, but a whole bowl of jello went down this lady's, uh, bazoom, and we haven't the slightest idea what to do about it!*

**bazoongies** AND **bawangos** *n.* a woman's breasts. (Usually objectionable.) ♦ *Every time she moved forward, even just a little, her bazoongies tended to stay behind,* *for just a second.* ♦ *With bawangos like that, she could be in the movies.*

**BCNU** [ˈbiˈsiˈənˈju] *tv.* Be seeing you. (An initialism. Appears in informal written contexts.) ♦ *Todd always closes his notes with "BCNU."*

**Be there or be square.** *sent.* Attend or be at some event or place or be considered uncooperative or not "with it." ♦ *There's a bunch of people going to be at John's on Saturday. Be there or be square.*

**beam up** *in.* to die. (From the television program *Star Trek.*) ♦ *Pete dead? I didn't think he was old enough to beam up.*

**bean 1.** *n.* the head. ♦ *I got a bump right here on my bean.* **2.** *tv.* to hit someone on the head. ♦ *The lady beaned me with her umbrella.* **3.** *n.* a human nipple, especially as seen through clothing. (From the shape.) ♦ *Gee, I can see her beans, even when it's not cold!*

**bean time** *n.* dinnertime. ♦ *I'm hungry. When's bean time around here?*

**bean-counter** *n.* a statistician; an accountant. ♦ *When the bean-counters get finished with the numbers, you won't recognize them.*

**bear cage** *n.* a police station. (Citizens band radio.) ♦ *Have you ever been in a country bear cage?*

**bear in the air** *n.* a police officer in an airplane or a helicopter. (Citizens band radio.) ♦ *They've got a bear in the air on duty in northern Indiana.*

**beasty** *mod.* [of a person] undesirable; yucky. (California.) ♦ *You are like, so like, beasty!*

**beat box** *n.* the person who provides the (verbal) rhythmic beat in a rap song. ♦ *What makes him sound so good is his beat box?*

**beat** one's **gums** *tv.* to waste time talking a great deal without results. ♦ *I'm tired of beating my gums about this stuff.*

**beat the rap** *tv.* to evade conviction and punishment (for a crime). ♦ *The police hauled Tom in and charged him with a crime. His lawyer helped him beat the rap.*

**beats me** *tv.* [the answer is] not known to me. (The emphasis is on *me*.) ♦ *I don't know the answer. Beats me!*

**beaut** [bjut] *n.* someone or something excellent, not necessarily beautiful. ♦ *This is a beaut of a day!*

**bedroom eyes** *n.* seductive eyes. ♦ *Beware of bedroom eyes. They mean trouble.*

**beema** *n.* a beemer; a BMW automobile. (Pop gangsta.) ♦ *Who's holding the kizzle to my beema?*

**been around (the block)** *phr.* sexually experienced. ♦ *He's just a kid. He hasn't been around the block yet.*

**been bobbing for fries** *phr.* [has] a really ugly face. (As if badly burned.) ♦ *Look at that face. Been bobbing for fries, I guess.*

**beer 1.** *in.* to drink beer. ♦ *Fred and Tom sat in there watching the game and beering and belching like two old whales.* **2.** *tv.* to get oneself drunk on beer. ♦ *I beered myself, but good.*

**beer goggles** [...'gɑglz] *n.* imaginary lenses (associated with too much beer) worn by someone for whom all persons of the opposite sex look very attractive. (Usually said about the eyes of males. See also **male blind-ness.** ♦ *See how Willy is looking at that dog? He's got his beer goggles on!*

**begathon** *n.* a televised appeal for contributions, especially as conducted by U.S. public television stations. ♦ *It seems like this station is one long begathon all year long.*

**beige** [beʒ] *mod.* boring; insipid. (California. See also **vanilla.**) ♦ *This day is way beige! Bag it!*

**belch** [bɛltʃ] *n.* beer, especially bad beer. ♦ *Pass the belch. Anything's good on a hot day.*

**belcher** [ˈbɛltʃɚ] **1.** *n.* a beer drinker. ♦ *Look at the belly on that belcher!* **2.** *n.* a hard drinker; a drunkard. ♦ *A couple of belchers wandered in about midnight. Other than that, the night is dead.*

**belly fiddle** *n.* a guitar. ♦ *Listen to that guy play that belly fiddle!*

**bench 1.** *tv.* to take someone out of a ball game. ♦ *The coach benched Jim, who injured his arm.* **2.** *tv.* to retire someone; to withdraw someone from something. ♦ *The manager benched the entire sales staff for cheating on their expense reports.*

**bench jockey** *n.* a player who sits on the bench and calls out advice. ♦ *The coach told all the bench jockeys to shut up.*

**bend the law** *tv.* to cheat a little bit without breaking the law. (Jocular.) ♦ *I didn't break the law. I just bent the law a little.*

**benda** *n.* a bender; a girl who copulates without much fuss. (Streets.) ♦ *He's always got a bunch of bendas following his ass around.*

**Benjamin** AND **Benji** *n.* a one hundred dollar bill. (Bearing a picture of Benjanin Franklin.) ♦ *You owe me two Benjamins!* ♦ *Here's the Benji I owe you.*

**best bud** *n.* a best buddy; a best friend. ♦ *Isn't Bill your best bud? Why are you so mad at him?*

**betty 1.** *n.* some fake drugs; a bad drug buy. ♦ *John's supplier slipped him some betty.* **2.** *n.* a good-looking girl or woman. (Usually **Betty**.) ♦ *Who's your new Betty, Bob?*

**bewottled** *mod.* alcohol intoxicated; tipsy. ♦ *Sam was so bewottled that he could hardly walk.*

**bezongas** *n.* a woman's breasts. (Usually objectionable.) ♦ *I've never seen so many definitely fine bezongas all in one place at the same time.*

**bi 1.** *n.* one of the biceps. (Bodybuilding. Typically **BI**. Usually plural.) ♦ *I have to work on my BIs and then build up my thighs.* **2.** *mod.* bisexual. ♦ *Suddenly she suspected that she was getting involved in some sort of strange bi activities.* **3.** *n.* a bisexual person. ♦ *This information is of interest only to bis and gays.*

**big blue** *n.* the stock of International Business Machines or the company itself. (Securities markets.) ♦ *Big blue led the market lower again today.*

**big board** *n.* the New York Stock Exchange. (Securities markets.) ♦ *On the big board, stocks were down again today, bringing the loss this week on the Dow to nearly 175 points.*

**big Dick** *n.* a ten rolled with the dice in craps. (Likely a veiled, punning reference to phallic length.) ♦ *Come, on! I want a big Dick! Baby needs shoes!*

**big fish** *n.* the boss; the leader. (Underworld.) ♦ *We took in the little guys, but the big fish got away.*

**big jab** *n.* a lethal injection used to carry out a death sentence. (Journalistic.) ♦ *Nearly 59 prisoners got the big jab in Texas this year.*

**big kahuna** *n.* the important person; the knowledgeable authority on some matter. (From the Hawai'ian word for "priest." Sometimes capitalized.) ♦ *Joe is the big kahuna around here when it comes to predicting stock market prices.*

**Big Mac attack** *n.* a sudden and desperate need for a Big Mac sandwich, a product of the McDonald's restaurant chain. (*Big Mac* is a protected trade name of McDonald's.) ♦ *I feel a Big Mac attack coming on!*

**big mouth 1.** *n.* a person who talks too much or too loudly; someone who tells secrets. (Also a term of address.) ♦ *Okay, big mouth! Shut up!* **2.** *tv.* to spread secrets around. ♦ *Why do you always big mouth everything around?*

**big stink** *n.* a major issue; a scandal; a big argument. ♦ *Don't make such a big stink about it.*

**bigass 1.** *n.* a person with very large buttocks. (Usually objectionable.) ♦ *Some bigass came in and broke the chair when he sat down.* **2.** *mod.* pertaining to someone who has very large buttocks. (Usually objectionable.) ♦ *Tell that bigass jerk to get out!* **3.** *mod.* pertaining to a person who is self-important, overbearing, or arrogant;

pertaining to anything having to do with arrogance. (Usually objectionable.) ♦ *Take your bigass ideas and go back where you càme from.* **4.** *mod.* really big. ♦ *Did you see that bigass SUV hit the little Honda?*

**biggie 1.** *n.* something or someone important. ♦ *As problems go, this one's a biggie.* **2.** *n.* copulation. (Usually with *the*.) ♦ *But I don't think I'm ready for the biggie.*

**big-ticket** *mod.* having to do with something expensive. ♦ *In a survey taken last month, heads of families said they were unwilling to put big-ticket items at the bottom of their shopping lists.*

**bike boys** *n.* cops; the police. ♦ *Look out! Here come the bike boys.*

**bimbo** ['bɪmbo] **1.** *n.* a clownlike person. ♦ *If that bimbo doesn't keep quiet, I'll bop him.* **2.** *n.* a giddy woman; a sexually loose woman. ♦ *Now that bimbo is a star in the movies!*

**bio break** *n.* a toilet break. (Contrived and euphemistic.) ♦ *She out of pocket for a bio break.*

**bird watcher** *n.* a girl watcher; someone, usually a man, who enjoys watching women go by. ♦ *You bird watchers should just mind your own business!*

**birdturd 1.** *n.* an obnoxious person. (Rude and derogatory.) ♦ *You silly birdturd. Wake up!* **2.** *mod.* stupid; obnoxious; lousy; worthless. (Usually objectionable.) ♦ *Of all the stupid, underhanded, birdturd tricks—this takes the cake!* **3.** *n.* bird dung, especially if dried. (Usually objectionable.) ♦ *There's birdturd on your shoe.*

**bison** *in.* to vomit. (Probably a play on **yak**.) ♦ *He stepped aside to bison in the bushes.*

**bit-bucket** *n.* the imaginary place where lost computer data goes. (Computers.) ♦ *I guess my data went into the bit-bucket.*

**bitch out** *in.* to complain. (Usually objectionable.) ♦ *You are always bitching out no matter how well off you are.*

**bitch slammer** *n.* a women's prison. (Streets.) ♦ *They threw her in the bitch slammer for three years.*

**bitch tits** *n.* gynecomastia; the development of breast tissue in the male. (From bodybuilding, in reference to breast development caused by steroids. Usually objectionable.) ♦ *If you don't let up on the gorilla juice, you'll get bitch tits.*

**bitchin'** AND **bitchen; bitching 1.** *mod.* excellent; great; classy. (Usually objectionable.) ♦ *This is a totally bitchin' pair of jeans!* **2.** *exclam.* Terrific! (Usually **Bitchin'!**) ♦ *Four of them? Bitchen!*

**Bite the ice!** *exclam.* Go to hell! ♦ *If that's what you think, you can just bite the ice!*

**biter 1.** *n.* a thief. ♦ *Some biter made off with my algebra book.* **2.** *n.* someone who copies someone else. (From the first sense.) ♦ *That's my steelo, you biter!*

**black and blue** *mod.* bruised, physically or emotionally. ♦ *I'm still black and blue from my divorce.*

**black and white** *n.* the police; a black and white police patrol car; any police car. ♦ *Call the black and whites. We got trouble here.*

**black-collar workers** *n.* people, usually affected, who wear black all the time. (Contrived. A play on *white-collar* and *blue-collar* workers.) ♦ *I hate to go over to the* *gallery. It's filled with black-collar workers. Reminds me of the Addams Family.*

**bladdered** *mod.* drunk, especially with a full bladder. ♦ *I'm really bladdered! Somebody drive me home?*

**blame shifting** *n.* a process in business and government wherein the blame for something bad is shifted from person to person. (A coinage that has appeal because it fills the need to express the concept succinctly.) ♦ *Can't we have a decent argument without your constant blame shifting?*

**blanco** *n.* a white person; a Caucasian. (From Spanish. Potentially derogatory.) ♦ *The blancos arrived in droves to enjoy our beaches.*

**blimp** *n.* a nickname for an obese person. ♦ *This enormous blimp managed to get on the plane but couldn't get into a seat.*

**blimp out** *in.* to overeat. ♦ *I love to buy a bag of chips and just blimp out.*

**bling-bling 1.** *n.* fancy jewelry, especially chains and the like that sparkle or tinkle when in motion. (Streets.) ♦ *All that bling-bling's gonna give you a sore neck!* **2.** *mod.* fancy or sparkly, from the glimmer of light. (Streets.) ♦ *Tiff! Your chains are so bling-bling!*

**blinky** AND **winky** ['blɪŋki AND 'wɪŋki] *n.* a device for smoking crack, a form of cocaine. (Drugs.) ♦ *Hold the blinky here and wait till I tell you.* ♦ *His winky blew up, and he's in the hospital.*

**blisterfoot** *n.* someone who walks a lot: a police patrol officer, a soldier, etc. ♦ *This blisterfoot puts his hand on my shoulder and says, "What's the rush, chum?"*

**blix** *tv.* to look at something; to glance at something. ♦ *She blixed my face and saw that I was so out of control!*

**block 1.** *n.* the head. ♦ *Try to get this stuff through your block before the test.* **2.** *n.* the auction block. ♦ *The painting went on the block and sold for nearly fifty-three million dollars.* **3.** *n.* a stupid person. ♦ *You silly block! Get out of the way.*

**blogging** *n.* making an entry into a weblog or blog = online diary. ♦ *When John said he was busy blogging, Sally said he should get a life!*

**blond moment** *n.* a lapse in thinking, something like a *senior moment.* ♦ *Sorry. I was having a blond moment. And that's hard for a redhead.*

**blooper** ['blupɚ] **1.** *n.* an embarrassing broadcasting error that must be bleeped or blooped out of the program. ♦ *There is a record you can buy that lets you hear the famous bloopers of the past.* **2.** *n.* an error. ♦ *That was a real blooper. Did you get fired?*

**blouse bunnies** *n.* the (covered) female breasts. ♦ *He couldn't keep his eyes off her busy little blouse bunnies.*

**blow a hype** *tv.* to overreact; to spaz out. ♦ *I was afraid she would blow a hype about the broken window.*

**blow beets** *tv.* to empty one's stomach; to vomit. ♦ *What was in that stew? I feel like I gotta blow beets.*

**blow cold** *in.* [for a person] to display disinterest. ♦ *The committee blew cold as my plan unfolded.*

**blow (one's) cookies** *tv.* to empty one's stomach; to vomit. ♦ *Okay, if any of you guys gotta blow your cookies or something, do it here, not inside!*

**blow** one's **own horn** AND **toot** one's **own horn** *tv.* to brag. ♦ *Gary sure likes to toot his own horn.* ♦ *Say something nice. I'm not one to blow my own horn.*

**blow snot rockets** AND **blow a snot rocket** *tv.* to blow gobs of nasal mucus from one nostril at a time by blocking off the other nostril with a thumb. ♦ *Bob is always blowing snot rockets! How crude!* ♦ *He tried to blow a snot rocket at the dog, but it kept right on barking.*

**blow** so's **mind 1.** *tv.* to impress someone; to overwhelm someone. ♦ *This whole business just blows my mind.* **2.** *tv.* [for a drug] to intoxicate someone. ♦ *This stuff will blow your mind.*

**blow the joint** *tv.* to get out of a place, probably in a hurry. (Underworld.) ♦ *Come on, let's blow the joint before there's trouble.*

**blow town** *tv.* to get out of town, probably in a hurry. (Underworld.) ♦ *I gotta pack and blow town. The cops are onto me.*

**blowed (away)** *mod.* alcohol or drug intoxicated. ♦ *I was so blowed away I couldn't see straight.*

**blown away 1.** *mod.* dead; killed. (Underworld.) ♦ *Four of the mob were already blown away when the cops got there.* **2.** AND **blown** *mod.* alcohol or drug intoxicated. ♦ *Whatever that pill was, Cecilia is totally blown away.* ♦ *She's blown and alone and making a groan.* **3.** *mod.* overwhelmed; greatly impressed. (Often with *with* or *by*.) ♦ *We were just blown away by your good words.*

**blue and white** *n.* a police car; the police. (Patterned on black and white and used in cities where the police cars are painted blue and white.) ♦ *A blue and white suddenly appeared, and I knew we were finished.*

**blue flu 1.** *n.* an imaginary disease afflicting police officers who call in sick during a work stoppage or slow-down. (Journalistic. Occurs where strikes are illegal.) ♦ *Another epidemic of the blue flu struck the city's police officers early today.* **2.** *n.* a hangover. ♦ *He was out late last night and has the blue flu.*

**blue screen of death** AND **BSOD** *phr. & comp. abb.* the blue computer screen that appears in early versions of Windows when Windows discovers a programming or operational error. ♦ *Every time I run that program I get the BSOD.* ♦ *No matter what program causes the blue screen of death, Bill Gates gets the blame.*

**blue suit** *n.* a police officer. (Usually plural.) ♦ *Watch out for the blue suits if you are going to drive this fast!*

**bluh** *n.* a buddy. (Streets.) ♦ *Yo, ma bluh!*

**boat anchor** *n.* a useless computer; anything heavy and useless. ♦ *Why don't you replace that boat anchor with a new model?*

**bobo** *mod.* drunk. ♦ *I think he's bobo. Get him out of here before he barfs.*

**bodacious** [bo'deʃəs] *mod.* assertive; audacious. ♦ *That is a bodacious plan, for sure.*

**bodega** *n.* a corner store; a local shop. (From a Spanish term for a wineshop, or simply borrowed from Hispanic speakers in the U.S.) ♦ *I picked this little thing up at my local bodega.*

**body shake** *n.* a shakedown of the body; a skin-search. (Underworld.) ♦ *They give everybody who passes through these doors a body shake.*

**boffo** ['bɑfo] **1.** *n.* a box-office hit; a successful play, musical, movie, etc. ♦ *The last one was a tremendous boffo, but we only broke even.* **2.** *mod.* successful; tremendous. ♦ *Another boffo success for Willy!*

**bogus beef** AND **bum beef** *n.* a false complaint or charge. ♦ *The cops took them in on a bogus beef.* ♦ *It's a bogus beef. I'll be back on the street in twenty minutes.*

**boheme** [bo'him] *n.* a (feminine) personal style consisting of no makeup, large baggy clothing, long skirts, and comfortable shoes. (Collegiate.) ♦ *Boheme is not you.*

**boil the ocean** *tv.* to waste one's time attempting to do the impossible. (See also plowing water.) ♦ *You're wasting my time. You might as well be boiling the ocean.*

**boink** *tv. & in.* to copulate [with] someone. (Usually objectionable.) ♦ *He said he boinked her twice.*

**boinkable** *mod.* suitable and agreeable for copulation. ♦ *See that babe? Wow, is she boinkable!*

**bojangling** *n.* acting stupid; acting like a stupid black. ♦ *Stop bojangling and settle down to work.*

**bone 1.** *n.* a trombone. (Musicians.) ♦ *She plays the bone like nobody's business.* **2.** Go to boner.

**bone factory 1.** *n.* a hospital. ♦ *After about two months in the bone factory, I was back on the job.* **2.** *n.* a cemetery. ♦ *I know I'll end up in the bone factory just like everyone else.*

**bone out** *in.* to leave. ♦ *It's time we boned out and got home.*

**boner 1.** *n.* a silly error; a gaffe. ♦ *What a boner! You must be embarrassed.* **2.** AND **bone** *n.* an erection. ♦ *He always gets a boner when he doesn't need it and never when he does.*

**bonk** [bɔŋk] **1.** *tv.* to strike one's head. ♦ *He bonked his head on the shelf.* **2.** *tv.* to strike someone on the head. ♦ *I bonked John on the head.* **3.** *tv. & in.* to copulate [with] someone. (Usually objectionable.) ♦ *She bonked him all night. At least that's what he said.*

**boobage** *n.* a woman's breasts; breasts in general. ♦ *Fantastic boobage! Know what I mean? Know what I mean?*

**boo-bird** ['bu'bɚd] *n.* a person who boos frequently at games or other public events. ♦ *The catcher turned and stared right at the loudmouthed boo-bird. Everybody knew what he was thinking.*

**boogie-board** ['bugibord OR 'bʊgibord] **1.** *n.* a surfboard. (California.) ♦ *Get your boogie-board out there in that tube.* **2.** *n.* a skateboard. (Teens.) ♦ *Can you imagine a boogie-board costing 600 dollars?*

**bookmark** *tv.* to make a note of something, mental or written. (From the concept of bookmarking web pages.) ♦ *That's a good thought. I'll bookmark that.*

**boom sticks** *n.* drumsticks. (Musicians.) ♦ *He always carries his boom sticks in his back pocket, and he beats on walls, radiators, desks—you name it.*

**boon** *in.* to leave the road in a car for the **boondocks**. ♦ *Tom has a four-wheel-drive so we can really boon!*

**boonies** *n.* a remote and undeveloped place. (From boondocks.) ♦ *He lives out there in the boonies.*

**bootleg 1.** *mod.* unauthorized or illegal [copy or something]; illegally obtained. ♦ *He crossed the state line to buy cigarettes and then returned by a back road with his bootleg smokes.* **2.** *n.* to sell unauthorized or illegal copies; to sell contraband. ♦ *They arrested the guy for bootlegging current movies on DVDs.*

**booty check** *n.* a search of the rectum, as when police look for drugs. ♦ *Willie got arrested and had a booty check since he was walking funny.*

**booty-cheddar** *n.* nonsense; bullshit. ♦ *I'm tired of listening to all your booty-cheddar.*

**bosom chums** AND **bosom friends** *n.* lice. ♦ *The old guy sat there scratching at his bosom chums.* ♦ *My bosom friends keep me awake all night.*

**boss dick** *n.* a cop; a police officer. (Streets.) ♦ *The boss dick slugged me in the face and said I should be more careful.*

**boss lady** *n.* the woman in charge. ♦ *You'll have to ask the boss lady.*

**boss man** *n.* the man in charge. ♦ *I guess the boss man is about ready to retire.*

**bottleache** ['badlek] *n.* a hangover; the delirium tremens. ♦ *I got a touch of the bottleache this morning.*

**bottom 1.** *n.* the buttocks. ♦ *My bottom is sore from sitting too long.* **2.** *n.* the second half of a baseball inning. ♦ *Wilbur hit a double-bagger in the bottom of the second.*

**3.** *tv.* to drink something to the bottom. ♦ *He bottomed the beer and ordered another one.*

**bouquet of assholes** *n.* an annoying or disgusting person or thing. (Rude and derogatory.) ♦ *Don't pay any attention to him. He's just another one of the bouquet of assholes you find around here.*

**bousta** *phr.* about to [do something]. (Streets.) ♦ *He's bousta go.*

**boxed** *mod.* dead; died. (The box is possibly a coffin.) ♦ *He's boxed. There's nothing that can be done.*

**boy-beater** *n.* a sleeveless shirt or undershirt allegedly for women or homosexuals. ♦ *They sat there looking macho in their tints and boy-beaters.*

**bozo filter** *n.* a setting on an Internet e-mail reader that will filter out selected annoying people. (Refers to bozo, a jerk.) ♦ *Welcome to my bozo filter, jerk!*

**brack-brain** ['brækbren] *n.* a fool. ♦ *The brack-brains in Washington have done it again!*

**brain-burned** AND **brain-fried** *mod.* brain-damaged from drugs. (Drugs.) ♦ *Man, you're gonna get brain-burned from this stuff.* ♦ *When he finally got totally brain-fried, he asked for help.*

**brass** so **off** *tv.* to make someone angry. (Primarily military. As angry as the "brass," or officers, might get about something.) ♦ *You really brass me off.*

**Bravo Sierra** *n.* nonsense; bullshit. (NATO Phonetic Alphabet.) ♦ *Sure, you're rich! What Bravo Sierra!*

**Break a leg!** *exclam.* Good luck! (A special theatrical way of wishing a performer good luck. Saying *good luck* is considered to be a jinx.) ♦ *"Break a leg!"* shouted the *stage manager to the heroine.*

**breaker 1.** *n.* a break dancer. (Break dancing is a rhythmic and energetic impromptu performance usually done by untrained urban youths.) ♦ *He is one of the best breakers in the city.* **2.** *n.* someone attempting to use a citizens band radio channel. ♦ *There's a breaker trying to use this channel. Let's drop down to eleven.*

**breakfast of champions** *n.* a first alcoholic drink of the day, taken in the morning, instead of breakfast. (Collegiate.) ♦ *He calls it the breakfast of champions. I call it a bad sign of something out of hand.*

**breeder** *n.* a nonhomosexual. (In a homosexual context.) ♦ *Don't invite Willy. He's a breeder.*

**brickhouse** *n.* a large-breasted woman. (A confused or euphemistic reference to built like a brick shithouse. Usually objectionable.) ♦ *Clara's a real brickhouse. I don't see how she stands up.*

**brights** *n.* the eyes. (From *bright eyes*.) ♦ *Don't you close your brights and look bored when I'm talking to you!*

**brim** *n.* a hat. ♦ *Man, that is one fine brim you got.*

**bring-down 1.** *n.* something that depresses someone. ♦ *The news was a terrible bring-down.* **2.** *n.* something that brings someone back to reality. ♦ *I have had one bring-down after another today.*

**brown bottle flu** *n.* a hangover or sickness from drinking. (Probably from beer, which is often sold in brown bottles.) ♦ *Wayne had a case of the brown bottle flu and didn't make the meeting.*

**brown hole 1.** *n.* the anus. (Usually objectionable.) ♦ *Sam Spade tried to kick Joel Cairo in the brown hole but missed.* **2.** *n.* to poke someone in the anus; to **goose** someone. (Usually objectionable.) ♦ *Fred brown-holed Tom on the stairway, and they had quite a fight.*

**brutal** *mod.* excellent; powerful. ♦ *Man, what a brutal tune!*

**bruva** *n.* a brother; my brother; my (black) buddy. (Black. Streets. May be social dialect only.) ♦ *Yo, bruva! Fo shizzle.*

**buckage** *n.* money. ♦ *Can you spare a little buckage until payday?*

**bucko** ['bəko] *n.* friend; pal. (Also a term of address. Can also be used with a sneer to convey contempt.) ♦ *Hey, bucko, come here a minute.*

**bud** [bəd] *n.* a Budweiser beer; any beer. ♦ *How 'bout one of them buds in a green bottle?*

**buddage** *n.* marijuana buds. ♦ *I'm out of buddage. Where's the man?*

**budget dust** *n.* a minor amount of money considering the size of the entire budget; money left over at the end of the budget year. ♦ *The amount is just budget dust, chump change! What's the big deal?*

**budhead** ['bədhɛd] *n.* a beer drinker. (See also **bud**.) ♦ *Here comes Charlie, my favorite budhead. How about a brew, Charlie?*

**buff(ed)** [bəft] *mod.* strong; muscular. ♦ *He has such buff legs! Does he have a job or does he just work out?*

**bug nut** *n.* a wire nut; a twist-on wire connector used to connect the ends of wires to complete a circuit. ♦ *Charlie, hand me a couple bug nuts, will ya?* ♦ *Hold them together, twist, and screw on the bug nut, see?*

**bugly** [ˈbəg li] *mod.* butt-ugly; really ugly. ♦ *I have never seen such a bugly guy in my life!*

**built like a brick shithouse 1.** *mod.* pertaining to a very strong and well-built person. (Usually refers to a male. Refers to the sturdiness of an outhouse [outdoor toilet] built of brick rather than the traditional wooden outhouse. Usually objectionable.) ♦ *Chuck is built like a brick shithouse. The only fat on him is where his brain ought to be.* **2.** *mod.* pertaining to a beautiful and curvaceous woman. (Refers to the imagined curving and uneven walls of an outhouse built hastily and carelessly of brick. This sense is a misinterpretation of the first sense. Usually objectionable.) ♦ *Look at that dame! She's really built like a brick shithouse.*

**bull session** *n.* a session of casual conversation. ♦ *The gals were sitting around enjoying a bull session.*

**bulldoze** *tv.* to apply pressure or force to get someone to do something. ♦ *You think you can bulldoze people into doing what you want!*

**bullets** *n.* nipples. ♦ *Nice boobage. Nice bullets.*

**bullyrag** [ˈbʊliræg] *tv. & in.* to harass someone. ♦ *Don't bullyrag me just because you're upset.*

**bum out 1.** *in.* to have a bad experience with drugs. (Drugs.) ♦ *I bummed out on angel dust.* **2.** *in.* to have any bad experience. ♦ *The test was horrible. I bummed out, for sure.*

bulldoze: "I hate when people bulldoze me."

**bummage** *n.* despair. (As in bummed (out).) ♦ *I got a load of bummage today. I'll get over it.*

**bumming** *mod.* down; depressed; suffering from something disagreeable. (Collegiate.) ♦ *I'm really bumming. I think I need somebody to talk to.*

**bump uglies** *tv.* [for two people] to copulate. ♦ *You been bumpin' uglies with Joannie again?*

**bumping 1.** *mod.* [of music] having a good beat. ♦ *Man, this music is bumping. I can feel the beat.* **2.** *mod.* crowded and busy. ♦ *This place is bumping. Let's sit in the corner, out of the way.* **3.** *mod.* really good; cool. ♦ *We had a bumping time at Tiff's last night.*

**bumping fuzzies** *n.* copulation. (The *fuzzies* refer to the participants' pelvic regions.) ♦ *She caught them bumping fuzzies in the pantry.*

**burb** [bəb] *n.* a suburb. (Usually plural.) ♦ *I've lived in the burbs all my life.*

**burger-flipper** *n.* a lowly hamburger cook in a fast-food restaurant. ♦ *If you drop out of school now, you'll end up being a burger-flipper for the rest of your life.*

**burn artist** *n.* someone who cheats or harms someone else; an informer. (Underworld.) ♦ *Never trust a known burn artist.*

**burn so down** *tv.* to humiliate someone. ♦ *You just want to burn down everybody to make yourself seem better.*

**burned 1.** *mod.* cheated; betrayed. ♦ *Man, did I get burned in that place!* **2.** *mod.* disappointed; humiliated; put down. ♦ *Ha! You're burned!* **3.** AND **burned up** *mod.* very angry. ♦ *I've never been so burned up at anyone.* ♦ *I am really burned! Totally burned!*

**burrnips** *mod.* cold. (Cold enough to make nipples harden.) ♦ *It's really cold, burrnips cold.*

**bush bitch** AND **bush pig** *n.* an ugly or unpleasant female. (Derogatory.) ♦ *Tom's been dating some bush pig from Adamsville.* ♦ *Shut your shitty mouth, you skanky bush bitch!*

**bust a grub** *tv.* to eat a meal. ♦ *Man, I'm starved. Let's go bust a grub.*

**bust a move** *tv.* to leave (a place). ♦ *Let's bust a move. Lots to do tomorrow.*

**bust (some) suds 1.** *tv.* to drink some beer. ♦ *Let's go out and bust some suds.* **2.** *tv.* to wash dishes. ♦ *You get into that kitchen and bust some suds to pay for your meal!*

**busta** *n.* a young kid trying to act tough; *buster.* (Streets. From or supported by Buster, the nickname.) ♦ *Sammy's just a busta. He won't get nowhere.*

**butch** [bʊtʃ] **1.** *n.* a physician. (Derogatory. From *butcher.*) ♦ *The butch at the infirmary was no help at all.* **2.** *mod.* virile and masculine. (In a homosexual context.) ♦ *Really, Clare. How butch!*

**butt thong** AND **butt floss** *n.* a thong bathing costume. (Mildly objectionable.) ♦ *You're not going to wear that butt thong in public are you?* ♦ *My mother called my bathing suit "butt-floss!"*

**butter face** *n.* a very ugly woman; a woman with everything just right *but her face.* ♦ *Nice shape, but she's a butterface.*

**butthead** *n.* a stupid or obnoxious person of either sex. (Also a term of address. Rude and derogatory.) ♦ *Don't be such a butthead!*

**butt-kicker** AND **ass-kicker** *n.* someone or something capable of defeating or surpassing all others. ♦ *That idea is a real butt-kicker.* ♦ *He is an ass-kicker, but he at least rewards us for putting up with him.*

**butt-munch** *n.* a despised male. (Usually objectionable.) ♦ *You dumb butt-munch! Why did you do that?*

**butt-ugly** *mod.* very ugly. (Usually objectionable.) ♦ *That is the most butt-ugly car I've ever seen.*

**buy it** *tv.* to die. ♦ *He lay there coughing for a few minutes, and then he bought it.*

**buzhie** ['buʒi] **1.** *n.* a middle-class person. (From *bourgeoisie.*) ♦ *I live in a neighborhood of buzhies.* **2.** *mod.*

middle-class. ♦ *I live in a buzhie house and drive a buzhie car.*

**buzzard meat** *n.* someone or something that is dead or outdated. ♦ *If you don't watch out, you're going to become buzzard meat!*

**buzzkill** *n.* someone or something that ruins enjoyment or pleasure; someone or something that ruins a buzz. ♦ *Oh, Willy! You're such a buzzkill!*

# C

**cabbage** *n.* money. (Originally underworld. See also spinach.) ♦ *How much cabbage you want for this heater?*

**caboose** [kə'bus] *n.* the buttocks. (From the name of the car at the end of a railroad train.) ♦ *You just plunk your caboose over there on the settee and listen up to what I have to tell you.*

**cackleberry** *n.* an egg. ♦ *You want cackleberries for breakfast?*

**caddy** ['kædi] *n.* a Cadillac automobile. ♦ *What I really want is a caddy. Keep your yuppie beemer.*

the **cage of anger** *n.* a prison. (Streets.) ♦ *The judge put JoJo into the cage of anger for a three-year stretch.*

**cakewalk** *n.* something very easy. ♦ *Nothing to it. It's a cakewalk.*

**calaboose** ['kæləbus] *n.* jail. (From a Spanish word.) ♦ *Are we going to tell what happened, or are we going to spend the night in the calaboose?*

**call 1.** *n.* a decision; a prediction. ♦ *The market behaved just as you said it would. Good call.* **2.** *tv.* to challenge someone. ♦ *I called him, but he ignored me.* **3.** *n.* the early effects of a drug; the beginning of a *rush*; a *rush*.

(Drugs.) ♦ *You may not get the call on this stuff for twenty minutes or more.*

**call hogs** *tv.* to snore really loudly. ♦ *Mike was calling hogs all night long and I got hardly a wink of sleep.*

**call so out** *tv.* to challenge someone to a fight. ♦ *Max wanted to call him out but thought better of it.*

**camel toes** *n.* a woman's vulva as it appears through blue jeans, especially jeans that have been pulled up too tight. ♦ *There's nothing attractive about camel toes.*

**campi** ['kæmpɑɪ] *n.* campuses. (The Latin plural of *campus* = field.) ♦ *I'll see you about the campi. Ciao!*

**can 1.** *n.* the head. ♦ *Jerry landed one on Frank's can. Frank crumpled.* **2.** *n.* toilet. ♦ *Restroom? Hell, I ain't tired! Where's the can?* **3.** *n.* the buttocks. (Usually objectionable.) ♦ *The guy slipped on the ice and fell on his can.* **4.** *n.* jail. (Usually with *the*.) ♦ *I had to spend the night in the can, but it wasn't too bad.* **5.** *tv.* to dismiss someone from employment. ♦ *The jerk canned everybody who played a part in the gag.* **6.** *n.* a car. ♦ *That's a good-looking can he's driving.* **7.** *n.* a breast. (Usually objectionable. Usually plural.) ♦ *Man, look at the cans on that dame!* **8.** *n.* a measurement of marijuana. (Drugs.) ♦ *How much do you want for a can?*

**cancel so's Christmas** *tv.* to kill someone; to destroy someone. (Underworld. The dead person will miss Christmas.) ♦ *If he keeps bugging me, I'm gonna cancel his Christmas.*

**candlelight** *n.* dusk; dawn. ♦ *I'll see you along about candlelight.*

**cane** AND **caine** *n.* cocaine. (Drugs.) ♦ *Even the kids can afford to buy cane now. The social problems of the twenty-first century are starting right here.*

**cannon** *n.* a gun; a revolver. (Underworld.) ♦ *Rocko pulled out his cannon and aimed it at Marlowe's throat.*

**can-shaker** *n.* a fund-raiser. (As if a person were holding a can for the solicitation of coins from passersby.) ♦ *Fred was a professional can-shaker for a museum. Maybe he has some ideas as to how we can raise some money.*

**caper** ['kepɚ] **1.** *n.* any stunt or event; a trick or a **scam.** ♦ *That little caper the kids did with the statue from the town square was a dandy.* **2.** *n.* a criminal job: theft, kidnapping, blackmail, etc. (Underworld.) ♦ *The black and whites pulled up right in the middle of the caper.*

**capital** *n.* cash; money. ♦ *I'm a little short of capital right now.*

**capper** ['kæpɚ] *n.* the climax or **clincher** of something. ♦ *The capper of the evening was when the hostess got lathered before midnight and couldn't celebrate the New Year.*

**carcass** ['kɑrkəs] *n.* one's body; a large or heavy body. ♦ *Put your carcass on a chair, and let's chew the fat.*

**carded** AND **proofed** *mod.* [of an ID card] examined to determine whether one has reached the legal drinking age. ♦ *Dave got carded at the party even though he is thirty and looks it.* ♦ *As soon as we were proofed, we got in and got some brews.*

**carebear** *n.* a nice person who is against violence and disputes. (Especially in the domain of computer games.

From the name of a set of lovable children's characters.) ♦ *These carebears don't want us to play the really good games!*

**case** so/sth **out** *tv.* to look someone or something over carefully, with a view to additional activity at a later time. ♦ *He cased out the fixtures to see which ones to replace.*

**cash cow** *n.* a dependable source of money; a good investment. ♦ *Mr. Wilson turned out to be the cash cow we needed to start our repertoire company.*

**cash** so **out** *tv.* to pay someone (off). ♦ *Come on, cash me out. I did the job. I want to go home.*

**casper** *mod.* gone; departed. (In the manner of Casper, the friendly ghost—a cartoon character.) ♦ *I'm casper. See you later.*

**catch 1.** *n.* a drawback. ♦ *Okay, that sounds good, but what's the catch?* **2.** *tv.* to view something; to attend something; to hear something. ♦ *Did you catch Gone with the Wind on TV?*

**catholic bagel** *n.* a nontraditional bagel made or flavored with cinnamon, blueberries, strawberries, etc. (Jocular.) ♦ *At breakfast, they had catholic bagels and sweet rolls.*

**cat-soup** ['kætsup] *n.* catsup; ketchup. ♦ *Do you want some cat-soup on your burger?*

**caucasian waste** *n.* worthless white people. (A play on (poor) white trash. Contrived.) ♦ *I'm not caucasian waste! I wouldn't ever live there!*

**celestial transfer** *n.* death. (Hospital, cruel, jocular word play.) ♦ *He's circling the drain. Almost ready for a celestial transfer.*

**cellular Macarena** *n.* the activity seen when a cell phone rings in public. ♦ *Beethoven's Fifth rang out and seven people started playing cellular Macarena.*

**chain(saw)** *tv.* to destroy something; to cut something up severely. ♦ *The senatorial committee tried to chainsaw the nominee, but the full senate voted for confirmation.*

**change the channel** *tv.* to switch to some other topic of conversation. ♦ *Let's change the channel here before there is a fight.*

**channel surfer** *n.* a person who practices channel hopping. ♦ *My husband is a confirmed channel surfer. I can't understand why he does it.*

**chapped** *mod.* angry; annoyed. ♦ *I was chapped. There was no way to get around it.*

**Charles 1.** *n.* cocaine. (Drugs.) ♦ *Is there a house where I can buy some Charles somewhere close?* **2.** *n.* a Caucasian. (Black. Not necessarily derogatory.) ♦ *And what is Charles gonna say about what you did to his car?*

**chart** *n.* a musical score. (Musicians. See also **map**.) ♦ *Come on, man! Look at the chart! You're making clinkers like hot cakes.*

**chas** AND **chez** [tʃæz AND tʃez] *n.* matches. (Collegiate. A clipping of *matches*.) ♦ *You got a couple of chez?*

**cheapie** *n.* a cheaply made article. (See also **el cheapo**.) ♦ *It broke. I guess it was a cheapie.*

**cheaters** *n.* sunglasses. (Formerly referred to all spectacles. See also **shades**.) ♦ *Get your cheaters on. The sun's really bright.*

**check that** *tv.* cancel that; ignore that (last remark). ♦ *At four, no, check that, at three o'clock this afternoon, a bomb exploded at the riverside.*

**check your six** *tv.* look behind you (where there may be danger). (See also **on your six**. Refers to six o'clock as being behind one, as if one were facing twelve o'clock.) ♦ *Check your six, bud. Some gangsta's getting close to your wallet.*

**cheddar** AND **chedda** *n.* money; cash. (Streets. From *cheddar*.) ♦ *Shizzle! I'm out of chedda.* ♦ *I'm totally out of cheddar. Can you loan me a Benji?*

**cheese-eater** *n.* an informer; a **rat fink**. (Rats eat cheese.) ♦ *Some cheese-eater called the clerk and warned her we were coming.*

**cheesing** *mod.* smiling. (From the practice of forcing people to smile by saying *cheese* when attempting to photograph them.) ♦ *Don't stand there cheezing. What do you want?*

**chevrolegs** *n.* the human legs, as used for transportation, instead of a car. (From the trade name, Chevrolet.) ♦ *I'll be late, because I only have my chevrolegs to get there—unless you want to give me a ride.*

**chew the cheese** *tv.* to vomit. ♦ *Fred's out in the bushes, chewing the cheese.*

**chewed** *mod.* abused. ♦ *After that argument at the office yesterday, I really felt chewed.*

**chi-chi** [ˈʃiʃi] *mod.* elegant. ♦ *Her living room is so chi-chi that you are afraid to go in.*

**chick magnet** Go to babe magnet.

**chick-flick** *n.* a movie intended for women and female interests. ♦ *I hate chick-flicks. It's a guy thing.*

**chickster** *n.* a cool and good-looking woman or chick. ♦ *She's one fine chickster.*

**chill so's action** *tv.* to squelch someone; to prevent someone from accomplishing something. ♦ *Just wait! I'll chill his action—just you wait.*

**chillaxin'** *n.* a period of relaxing and chilling. (Contrived.) ♦ *What do you mean, I'm chillaxin'? I'm just taking it easy.*

**chillin'** *mod.* great; excellent. ♦ *Everybody there was chillin'.*

**Ching!** AND **Ka-ching!** *exclam.* the sound of a cash register, said to indicate money or imply a financial motive or success. ♦ *Just got another big order. Ka-ching!* ♦ *Tell, me what's important, dude. Ching! Right?*

**choad** AND **chode** **1.** *n.* the penis. (There are numerous ideas about the origin of this (these). They may not have the same origin. One possibility is French *chaud* = hot.) ♦ *Quit scratching your chode.* **2.** *n.* a real or imaginary penis that is short and squat. ♦ *You wimp! Get out and take your chode with you!* **3.** *n.* a jerk or oafish male. (Similar to prick, etc. This is probably the most common, current use.) ♦ *You stupid chode!* **4.** *n.* the perineum; the flesh between the genitals region and the anus. ♦ *A mountain bike team called the "Choad Chafers" won the championship.*

**choke 1.** *in.* [for a computer] to fail to take in information being fed to it. (Computers.) ♦ *If you don't have your modem and your software set the same way as the host, your machine will choke.* **2.** *in.* to panic before or during a test. (From *choke up*.) ♦ *She always chokes during a test.*

**choker 1.** *n.* a cigarette; a cigarette butt. ♦ *Put that damn choker out in my house!* **2.** *n.* a necktie. ♦ *Hey, Tom! That's a classy new choker you're wearing!*

**chones 1.** *n.* the testicles. (From Spanish *cojones*. Usually objectionable.) ♦ *You look at me that way again, and you will be saying good-bye to your chones.* **2.** *n.* bravado. (Usually objectionable.) ♦ *Man, has he got chones!*

**chooms** *n.* the testicles. (Usually objectionable.) ♦ *He got hit in the chooms in the football game.*

**chop-shop** *n.* a place where stolen cars are cut or broken up into car parts for resale. ♦ *The state is cracking down on these chop-shops.*

**chronic** *n.* very high quality marijuana containing lots of THC. (Probably from the association of THC with the use of marijuana in cases of chronic pain.) ♦ *Where can I get some genuine chronic?*

**chub(by)** *n.* an erection. (Usually objectionable.) ♦ *He always gets a chubby when he doesn't need it and never when he does.*

**Chuch!** *interrog. & exclam.* a general emphatic question tag meaning, roughly, *Right?*, and calls for the response Chuch! = Right! (Streets. Possibly derived from *church* implying truth.) ♦ *We're going to settle this now! Chuch?*

**chuck** sth **down** *tv.* to eat something very quickly. ♦ *Don't just chuck your food down. Enjoy it!*

**chuckers** AND **chucks** *n.* a great hunger; an enormous appetite. (Usually with *the*.) ♦ *We've got three impatient young boys with the chuckers! Feed 'em!* ♦ *Oh, man, I really got the chucks. What time is chow?*

**chug** *in. & tv.* [for one person] to drink something, usually beer, quickly and in large volumes. ♦ *He chugged three in a row, and they came right back up again.*

**chump change** *n.* a small amount of money; the kind of salary or amount of money a **chump** would work for. ♦ *I refuse to work for chump change! I want a real job.*

**Ciao, for now.** AND **C4N** *phr. & comp. abb.* Good-bye for the present. (*Ciao* is Italian. Phrase is current English.) ♦ *See U L8R. C4N.* ♦ *That's all for the moment. Ciao, for now.*

**circling (the drain)** *tv. & in.* to be in the final process of dying; to be in extremis. (Jocular but crude hospital jargon.) ♦ *Get Mrs. Smith's son on the phone. She's circling the drain.*

**civil serpent** *n.* a civil servant. ♦ *You have no idea the kinds of things "civil serpents" have to put up with.*

**clanked** *mod.* exhausted; pooped. ♦ *I'm really clanked, man. Gotta take a rest.*

**clay pigeon** *n.* a gullible person; a **pigeon**. (Underworld.) ♦ *We need a clay pigeon to divert attention from the snatch.*

**clear 1.** *mod.* alcohol intoxicated. ♦ *He was clear. You know, polluted.* **2.** *mod.* [of liquor] undiluted; neat. ♦ *I like mine clear with just one ice cube.* **3.** *tv.* to earn a specific net amount of money. ♦ *We just want to clear a decent profit. Nothing greedy.*

**click (with so)** *in.* to catch on with someone; to intrigue someone; to become popular with someone. ♦ *Sam and Mary are getting along fine. I knew they'd click.*

**climb 1.** *n.* a marijuana cigarette. (Drugs. The means to a high.) ♦ *I need a climb to set me straight.* **2.** *tv.* to scold someone. ♦ *The boss climbed Harry for being late.*

**clinker 1.** *n.* a mistake; (in music) a misplayed note. ♦ *Look at the score, man! That series of clinkers just isn't there.* **2.** *n.* a worthless person or thing. (From the term for a cinder.) ♦ *Ralph has turned out to be a real clinker. We'll have to pink slip him.*

**clobbered** *mod.* alcohol intoxicated. ♦ *He's the kind of guy who goes home and gets clobbered after work.*

**clock** *tv.* to earn, score, or total up someone or something. (As if the person or thing gained were being metered or clocked.) ♦ *Sam clocked a date with Sally, and is he ever proud!*

**close combat sock** *n.* a condom. ♦ *I'm all equipped with money and close combat socks.*

**closet** *mod.* secret; concealed. (Alludes to something being hidden in a closet.) ♦ *Marty is a closet chocolate fiend.*

**cluck** AND **kluck** [klək] *n.* a stupid person; a person as stupid as a chicken. ♦ *Why did they send me a dumb* *cluck to do this work?* ♦ *You silly kluck! Why'd you do that?*

**clucky** *mod.* stupid; oafish. ♦ *The plan you submitted to this office was rejected by the policy committee. They noted that it was the cluckiest idea they had ever seen.*

**clunky** *mod.* ponderous and inefficient. ♦ *I got rid of all the clunky stuff. Now it's lean and mean.*

**cluster fuck 1.** *n.* an act of group rape. (Also **Charlie Foxtrot** from the initials **CF**. Usually objectionable.) ♦ *Look at her! She's just asking for a cluster fuck.* **2.** *n.* any event as riotous as an act of group rape. (Figurative on sense 1. The same allusion as sense 1.) ♦ *This goddamn day has been one long cluster fuck!*

**coaster** *n.* someone who lives near the ocean on the coast. (California.) ♦ *Tiffany is a coaster now, but she was born, like, somewhere else.*

**cocked** *mod.* drunk. ♦ *She's too cocked to drive. You drive her home.*

**cocksocket** *n.* the vagina. ♦ *My little puck bunny has the sweetest cocksocket.*

**code brown** *n.* a fecal accident. (Jocular word play based on a hospital's PA announcements of various color codes.) ♦ *Code brown on third floor east.*

**code yellow** a urinary accident. (Jocular word play based on a hospital's PA announcements of various color codes.) ♦ *Whoops. Code yellow. Change the sheets and the mattress.*

**coin** *n.* money. ♦ *He made a lot of coin on the last picture.*

**cold 1.** *mod.* [stopping something] suddenly and totally.
♦ *I stopped cold—afraid to move further.* **2.** *mod.* dead.
♦ *This parrot is cold—pifted!* **3.** *mod.* not good. ♦ *The lecture was cold and dull.* **4.** *mod.* excellent. (Very **cool**.)
♦ *That last pitch was cold, man.*

**cold call** *tv.* to call a sales prospect from a list of persons one has never met. ♦ *Things have to be pretty bad when the senior brokers at a major house have to cold call people to get business.*

a **cold piece of work** *n.* a person who is difficult to deal with. ♦ *Buddy, you are a cold piece of work.*

**coli** AND **broccoli** ['kɑli, 'brɑk ə li] *n.* marijuana. (Drugs. From *broccoli*.) ♦ *Who got into my stash and took the coli?* ♦ *Don't forget your broccoli! Love them vegetables!*

**comboozelated** [kəm'buzəledəd] *mod.* alcohol intoxicated. (Collegiate.) ♦ *I believe I am just a little comboozelated.*

**come down hard on** SO *in.* to scold someone; to punish someone severely. ♦ *Joe's parents came down hard on him when they learned he had been suspended from school.*

**come on to** SO **1.** *in.* to make advances to a person. ♦ *She didn't even know he was coming on to her, till they got to his place.* **2.** *in.* to try to get someone to respond romantically or sexually. ♦ *She was just starting to come on to me when her parents came home.* **3.** *in.* to begin to become friendly. ♦ *After a few minutes, they began to come on to each other.*

**comer** ['kəmɚ] *n.* someone with a bright future. ♦ *Fred is a real comer. You'll be hearing a lot about him.*

**comma-counter** *n.* a pedantic person; a pedantic copy editor. ♦ *When you need a proofreader, you need a comma-counter.*

**company man** *n.* a man who always sides with his employers. ♦ *Ken's a company man—he'll always take management's side.*

**conehead 1.** *n.* a fool; an oaf. ♦ *You can be pretty much of a conehead yourself sometimes, you know.* **2.** *n.* an intellectual; a pointy-head. ♦ *They build fences around universities to keep the coneheads in.*

**cones** *n.* the breasts; female breasts. ♦ *She ain't much in the cones department.*

**confuckulated** *mod.* confused and messed up. (Usually objectionable.) ♦ *I'm so confuckulated! Let me think this through.*

**cookie pusher 1.** *n.* a bootlicker; someone who flatters other people for self-serving motives. ♦ *When you've got a whole office full of cookie pushers, there's always someone to take you to lunch.* **2.** *n.* a lazy do-nothing. ♦ *I'm just looking for a cookie pusher to fire today.*

**cool** so **out** *tv.* to calm someone; to appease someone. ♦ *The manager appeared and tried to cool out everybody, but that was a waste of time.*

**cooler** *n.* jail. (Usually with *the.*) ♦ *Do you want to talk, or do you want to spend a little time in the cooler?*

**coolth** *mod.* coolness. (Old. The mate to *warmth.*) ♦ *Close the door! You're letting all the coolth out of the fridge.*

**cop a tube** *tv.* to catch a perfect tubular wave. (Surfers.) ♦ *Mark—as drunk as all get out—said he was gonna go out and cop a tube.*

**cop onto** sth *in.* to understand or become aware of something. ♦ *I think I'm copping onto the significance of this at last.*

a **copy** *n.* a piece, as with an item produced. ♦ *We sell the toy at $14 a copy.*

**cords** *n.* a basketball net. ♦ *They cut the cords down after the game.*

**corn** *n.* money. ♦ *I need some corn to pay the rent.*

**corn squabble** *n.* a fight. (Perhaps referring to chickens fighting over corn.) ♦ *Stop this silly corn squabble and let's try to talk this through.*

**cornfed** *mod.* rural; backward; unsophisticated. ♦ *I enjoy her honest, cornfed humor.*

**couch potato** *n.* a lazy, do-nothing television watcher. (See also **sofa spud.**) ♦ *If there was a prize for the best couch potato, my husband would win it.*

**cow** *n.* a fat or ugly woman. (Cruel.) ♦ *Wouldn't you think a cow like that would go on a diet?*

**cowboy** *n.* a reckless and independent man; a reckless driver. (Also a term of address.) ♦ *Come on, cowboy, finish your coffee and get moving.*

**coyote-ugly** ['kaɪɔt 'əgli ᴏʀ 'kaɪoti 'əgli] *mod.* extremely ugly. (Crude, cruel, and potentially offensive. Said of people. Supposedly, if one woke up and found one's arm around a **coyote-ugly** person, one would chew off one's arm—in the manner of a coyote escaping from a steel-jaw trap—rather than pull it back away from this person.) ♦ *Is that your pet monkey, or is your date just coyote-ugly?*

**crack a tube** *tv.* to open a can of beer. ♦ *Why don't you drop over this evening, and we'll crack a few tubes?*

**crack some suds** *tv.* to drink some beer. ♦ *Let's go out tonight and crack some suds.*

**crackbrain** *n.* a fool; stupid oaf. ♦ *Did you hear about the crackbrain who said he found part of the sky floating in the lake?*

**crack-rack** *n.* an extra seat on a motorcycle, behind the driver. (Refers either to the anatomy of the buttocks placed thereon, or to the genital anatomy of a female passenger.) ♦ *Get on the crack-rack, and I'll give you a ride.*

**cranking** *mod.* exciting; excellent. ♦ *We had a massively cranking time at your place.*

**crapped (out)** *mod.* dead; finished. (Not prenominal. From dice, not from the other senses of **crap**.) ♦ *After a serious encounter with a rattlesnake, my two dogs were crapped by dawn.*

**crash cart** *n.* a nickname for the hospital cart that carries equipment used to attempt to restore a heartbeat, such as a defibrillator. ♦ *Get the crash cart to third west.*

**crasher** *n.* a person who attends a party uninvited. ♦ *The crashers ruined the party, and my dad called the cops.*

**crater 1.** *n.* an acne scar. ♦ *Walter was always sort of embarrassed about his craters.* **2.** *in.* to collapse and go down as with a falling stock price. ♦ *The stock cratered and probably won't recover for a year or two.*

**crater-face** AND **pizza-face; pizza-puss; zit-face** *n.* a person with acne or many acne scars. (Intended as jocular. Rude and derogatory.) ♦ *I gotta get some kind of medicine for these pimples. I'm getting to be a regular crater-face.* ♦ *I don't want to end up a zit-face, but I love chocolate!*

**credenzaware** *n.* reports that sit on an executive's credenza, primarily for show. (Contrived.) ♦ *Everything I send her ends up as credenza ware.*

**crips** *n.* marijuana. ♦ *This ain't crips; it's alfalfa.*

**crisco** ['krɪsko] *n.* a fat person. (Cruel. Also a rude term of address. The brand name of a baking shortening.) ♦ *Some crisco came in and ordered ten large fries.*

**cromagnon** [kro'mægnən] *n.* an ugly male. (Collegiate. Essentially *caveman*. From *Cro-Magnon*, the ancestor of the current human species. See also **neanderthal**, which is a variety of man presumed to be uglier and less like modern man.) ♦ *Who is that cromagnon you were with last night?*

**cros** *n.* Velcro. (A protected trade name for hook and loop fasteners.) ♦ *His pants pocket has cros, and I get to his wallet.*

**crotch rocketeer** *n.* a motorcycle driver; one who drives a **crotch-rocket**. ♦ *None of these crotch rocketeers is wearing a helmet.*

**crotch-cobra** *n.* the penis. (Usually objectionable.) ♦ *He held his hands over his crotch-cobra and ran for the bedroom.*

**crotch-rocket** *n.* a motorcycle. (For some, only foreign motorcycles are so called.) ♦ *I can buy a nice car for less than you paid for that crotch-rocket.*

**crud 1.** *n.* any nasty substance. (An old form of the word *curd*.) ♦ *There's some crud on your left shoe.* **2.** *n.* junk; stuff; personal possessions. ♦ *Get your crud outa my way, will you!* **3.** *n.* a repellent person. (Rude and derogatory.) ♦ *Don't be such a crud!*

**crunchers** *n.* the feet. ♦ *New shoes can be hard on your crunchers.*

**crunchie** *n.* a soldier; a marching infantry soldier. (Military. See also **crunchers**.) ♦ *Crunchies have a pretty hard life.*

**crunk** AND **krunk 1.** *mod.* wild; crazy; out of control. (The word itself has many uses, each freshly misunderstood or derived from earlier senses. It could be a blend of *crud + junk, crazy + drunk,* or other words, such as being a pseudo past participle of **crank** cocaine. There is an "energy drink" called crunk, and it claimed that the whole phenomenon is related to an extremely energetic Atlanta hip-hop star.) ♦ *He's acting crunk. Don't let him drive!* **2.** *mod.* drunk. ♦ *They went out and got totally crunk to celebrate.* **3.** *mod.* hip; cool; totally excellent. ♦ *Man, this CD is crunk!* **4.** *in.* to get excited or hyped up. ♦ *This brother is really crunking.*

**crutch 1.** *n.* a car. (Streets.) ♦ *That's one fine crutch you got here, Bud.* **2.** *n.* a device to hold a marijuana cigarette butt. ♦ *Here's a crutch so you can finish your smoke.*

**cry hughie** ['kraɪ 'hjui] *tv.* to empty one's stomach; to vomit. ♦ *He is in the john crying hughie.*

**crying towel** *n.* someone or something used to comfort someone. ♦ *It's so sad. I guess I really need a crying towel today.*

**crystal 1.** *n.* crystallized cocaine. (Drugs.) ♦ *Crystal—an older name for crack—was a favorite many years ago.* **2.** *n.* liquid Methedrine in glass ampoules. (Drugs.) ♦ *I hear that Willy's shooting crystal. Is that true?*

**crystals** *n.* the testicles. (From *crystal balls*.) ♦ *He got hit right in the crystals. It was real embarrassing, as well as painful.*

**cuddle bunny** *n.* a female lover. ♦ *All you want is a cuddle bunny with big tits! Grow up, Maxwell Wilson!*

**cup of tea** *n.* something preferred or desired. (Often negative.) ♦ *Driving children around all afternoon is not my cup of tea.*

**curtains** *n.* death. (Underworld.) ♦ *Okay, Marlowe, this time it's curtains.*

**cut no ice (with so)** *tv.* to have no influence on someone; to fail to convince someone. ♦ *I don't care who you are. It cuts no ice with me.*

**cut** one's **wolf loose** *tv.* to go on a drinking bout; to get drunk. ♦ *I'm gonna go out and cut my wolf loose tonight.*

**cut so a break** AND **cut so some slack** *tv.* to give someone a break; to allow someone a reprieve from the consequences of an action. ♦ *Come on! Cut me a break! I won't do it again!* ♦ *Cut me some slack and I'll be sure to pay you all I owe in a month.*

**Cut the comedy!** *exclam.* Get serious!; Stop acting silly! ♦ *That's enough, you guys. Cut the comedy!*

**cut to the chase** *in.* to focus on what is important; to abandon the preliminaries and deal with the major points. ◆ *After a few introductory comments, we cut to the chase and began negotiating.*

**cut (up)** *mod.* having well-defined abdominal muscles. ◆ *Andy works hard to try to get a gut that's cut.*

**cuts** *n.* sharply defined musculature, especially in the abdominal area. ◆ *Look at the cuts on that guy! What great abs!*

# D

**dairies** *n.* the breasts. ♦ *Fine dairies on that one!*

**damage** *n.* the cost; the amount of the bill (for something). ♦ *As soon as I pay the damage, we can go.*

**Damn straight!** *exclam.* You are absolutely right!; Yes!; Right on! ♦ *Am I mad? Damn straight!*

**dank** [dæŋk] **1.** *mod.* very good. ♦ *We stopped for a while in this real dank little bistro on the main boulevard.* **2.** *mod.* very bad. ♦ *Class was so dank today. I thought I would die of terminal boredom.* **3.** *n.* potent, moist marijuana. (Said to be stored away from light.) ♦ *I'll take dank any day.*

**dap** [dæp] *mod.* well-dressed. (From *dapper.*) ♦ *Man, you look so dap!*

**darb** [dɑrb] *n.* an excellent person or thing. ♦ *Carl is a real darb. I'm glad to know him.*

**dead from the neck up 1.** *mod.* stupid. (With a *dead* head.) ♦ *She acts like she is dead from the neck up.* **2.** *mod.* no longer open to new ideas. ♦ *Everyone on the board of directors is dead from the neck up.*

**dead president** *n.* a piece of U.S. paper money. (Refers to the pictures of presidents on the bills.) ♦ *This silly magazine costs three dead presidents!*

damage: "What's the damage?"

**deadcat bounce** *n.* a small, knee-jerk rally in one of the financial markets. (A dead cat—or any other animal—will bounce only slightly after being dropped. Refers to a stock index or security price that bounces up only slightly after a precipitous fall. Securities market.) ♦ *The whole market gave only a deadcat bounce after the string of losses this last week.*

**deaded 1.** *mod.* spent; used up; done for; **cashed.** ♦ *All my goodwill is gone. Cashed. Deaded.* **2.** *tv.* to kill someone. ♦ *The gang deaded him with a deuce-deuce.*

**deadneck** *n.* a stupid person. ♦ *Who's the deadneck who painted the fence purple?*

**decent** *mod.* good; very good. ♦ *This is some pretty decent jazz.*

**deduck** ['didək] **1.** *n.* a tax deduction. (From *deduct.*) ♦ *I need a few more deducks this year.* **2.** AND **duck** *n.* a deduction from one's paycheck. ♦ *More of my pay goes to deducks than I get myself.* ♦ *What's this duck for?*

**deduction** *n.* a child. (Actually a child is an exemption on the U.S. income tax return.) ♦ *How many little deductions do you have running around your home?*

**def** [dɛf] **1.** *mod.* better; cool. (Originally black. From *definitive*.) ♦ *Man, that yogurt is def!* **2.** *mod.* definitely. ♦ *This is def the best there is.*

**defrosted** *mod.* even with someone who has insulted, embarrassed, or angered oneself. ♦ *He yelled at her till he was defrosted, and then things settled down.*

**déjà moo** *n.* [tired] old bullshit. (Based on *déjà vu*, and the *moo* brings in the bovine aspect. Contrived, but admirable nonetheless.) ♦ *Are you still peddling that nonsense? Nothing but déjà moo, all over again.*

**delish** [dəˈlɪʃ] *mod.* delicious. ♦ *Oh, this cake is just delish.*

**delts** [dɛlts] *n.* the deltoid muscles. (Bodybuilding.) ♦ *Look at the delts on that dame!*

**desk jockey** *n.* someone who works at a desk in an office. (Patterned on **disk jockey**.) ♦ *I couldn't stand being a cooped-up desk jockey.*

**deuce** [dus] **1.** *n.* the devil. (Always with *the*.) ♦ *I'll knock the deuce out of you if you come around here again.* **2.** *n.* the two in playing cards. ♦ *If I could only get a deuce.* **3.** *n.* two dollars. ♦ *Can you loan me a deuce till payday?* **4.** *n.* a two-year prison sentence. (Underworld.) ♦ *The DA made sure that Mooshoo got more than a deuce.* **5.** *n.* a table for two. ♦ *Give the next couple the deuce over in the corner.*

**deuce-deuce** *n.* a .22-caliber pistol. (Streets.) ♦ *My buddy popped his uncle with a deuce-deuce.*

**dialog** *tv.* to attempt to deceive someone; to attempt to seduce someone. ♦ *Ron was dialoging this dame when her brother came in.*

**dicey** ['daɪsi] *mod.* touchy; chancy; touch and go. ♦ *Things are just a little dicey right now.*

**dick for** *n.* a person dumb enough to ask "What's a dick for?" (Jocular and contrived. Usually objectionable.) ♦ *The guy's a real dick for.*

**dick smack** *n.* a moron; a stupid jerk. (Possibly a reference to masturbation.) ♦ *You loony dick smack! Get out of my face!*

**dickwad** *n.* a stupid and ineffective male. (Possibly a reference to semen.) ♦ *What a dickwad! Beat it!*

**dickweed** *n.* a stupid and ineffective male. ♦ *He's nothing but a pathetic dickweed!*

**diesel** ['dizl̩] *mod.* really good. ♦ *I am set for a diesel evening and I intend to enjoy it.*

**diff** [dɪf] *n.* difference. ♦ *Aw, come on! What's the diff?*

**differential** *n.* the buttocks; the rear (end). (From the name of the device that joins the axle to the driveshaft in motorized vehicles.) ♦ *You're walking like there's something wrong with your differential.*

**digits** *n.* [someone's] telephone number. ♦ *Give me your digits, and I'll call you.*

**dim** *n.* the evening; the night. (Streets.) ♦ *Where'll you be this dim?*

**dime store** *n.* an establishment that is chaotic because of its small scale. ♦ *I can't stand this dime store anymore. This is no way to run a law firm.*

**dinero** [dɪˈnɛro] *n.* money. (Spanish.) ♦ *I don't have as much dinero as I need, but other than that, I'm doing okay.*

**dingus 1.** *n.* a thing or gadget. ♦ *I have a little dingus that helps me clean venetian blinds.* **2.** AND **dingy** *n.* the penis; the male *thing*. (Usually objectionable.) ♦ *Jimmy, shake your dingus and put it away!*

**dipshit 1.** AND **diphead; dipstick** *n.* an oaf; a jerk. (Rude and derogatory.) ♦ *Look, dipstick, I'm in a hurry.* ♦ *Don't be such a diphead!* **2.** *mod.* pertaining to someone or something obnoxious, stupid, or offensive. (Usually objectionable.) ♦ *Here's another one of his dipshit ideas.*

**dipwad** [ˈdɪpwad] *n.* a jerk; a nerd. (Euphemistic for dipshit.) ♦ *If you weren't a big dipwad, you would give me a hand with this.*

**dirtbag** *n.* a low, worthless person. ♦ *Spike is a slimy dirtbag, and I want him put away for good.*

**discipline** *n.* drugs. ♦ *She smokes this stuff she calls discipline. Smells like pot to me.*

**discombobulated** AND **discomboobulated** [dɪskəmˈbɑbjəledəd AND dɪskəmˈbubjəledəd] **1.** *mod.* confused. ♦ *I get completely discombobulated when I think of figures that big.* **2.** *mod.* alcohol intoxicated. ♦ *From the way she is walking, I'd say she is discombobulated.*

**dis(s)** *tv.* to belittle someone; to show disrespect for someone. (From *disrespect*.) ♦ *Please stop dissing my little sister. She didn't do any of those things.*

**dis(s) (on** SO) ['dɪs...] *in.* to belittle [someone]; to show disrespect [for someone]. (From *disrespect*.) ♦ *Gary is such a complainer. All he does is diss.*

**divot** ['dɪvət] *n.* a toupee; a partial toupee. ♦ *His divot slipped, but no one laughed.*

**do a bean count** *tv.* to stare at female breasts, looking for hard nipples. (A play on *bean-counter*.) ♦ *He thinks that early spring is a great time for a bean count. No jackets and cool breezes!*

**do a fade** *tv.* to leave; to sneak away. ♦ *It's time for me to do a fade.*

**do a number on** SO AND **do a job on** SO (From *do a number on sth*.) *tv.* to harm or deceive someone. ♦ *The prof did a number on me because of my term paper.* ♦ *My local friendly plumber did a job on me cleaning out my drain.*

**do a number on** sth **1.** *tv.* to urinate or defecate on something. ♦ *Billy did a number on the bathroom floor.* **2.** *tv.* to damage or ruin something; to destroy something. ♦ *The truck really did a number on my car.*

**do some fine coin** *tv.* to make a large sum of money. ♦ *When I get my big break, I'm going to do some fine coin.*

**do the drink thing** *tv.* to drink alcohol heavily. ♦ *He's been doing the drink thing quite a lot lately.*

**doc(s)-in-a-box** *n.* a walk-in emergency health care center, as found in shopping centers. ♦ *I was cut and went immediately to the docs-in-a-box in the mall.*

**dode** [dod] *n.* a nerd; a simpleton. ♦ *My roommate is a loser. I was afraid I'd end up with a dode.*

**dodge** [dɑdʒ] *n.* a swindle; a **scam**; a deception. ♦ *What sort of dodge did you get flimflammed with?*

**dog meat** *n.* a dead person. (Typically in a threat.) ♦ *Make one move, and you're dog meat.*

**dog's mother** *n.* a bitch; a bitchy person. (Euphemistic.) ♦ *If Sally insists on being a dog's mother on this matter, I'll tell her what I think of her.*

**dog-log** *n.* a section of dog feces. (Contrived.) ♦ *I think I stepped in a pile of dog-logs. Yuck!*

**dognutz** *n.* a friend; a buddy. (Streets.) ♦ *Come on, dognutz. Let's get moving.*

**doink** *tv.* to steal something. ♦ *We doinked a few apples from the cart.*

**doje** *n.* the penis. (Probably from one of the many vague words for *thing*, such as *doogie*.) ♦ *Stop scratching your doje.*

**domino** *n.* a one-hundred-dollar bill. ♦ *How many dominos is that going to cost?*

**done over** *mod.* beat; outscored. ♦ *Bruno felt that Frank would get the idea if he was done over a little.*

**donorcycle** *n.* a motorcycle. (Refers to the availability of donor organs after a motorcycle accident.) ♦ *Guess what happens when you ride a donorcycle without a helmet?*

**don't give a rip** *tv.* don't really care at all. ♦ *Go ahead! Ruin your life! I don't give a rip.*

**doofer** AND **dufer** ['dufɚ] *n.* a (found or borrowed) cigarette saved for smoking at another time. (It will *do for later*.) ♦ *He takes two fags, one to smoke and a dufer.*

**doofus** AND **duffis** ['dufəs] *n.* a jerk; a nerd. ♦ *Get out, doofus!* ♦ *My roommate is a duffis and I'm tired of putting up with her.*

**dook** AND **duke** [duk] **1.** *mod.* really bad. (Probably related to *duky.*) ♦ *This day was really dook!* **2.** *in.* to defecate. ♦ *Mom, I gotta dook.* **3.** to perform anal sex. (Offensive if understood.) ♦ *The dude wanted to dook me!*

**doowacky** ['duʍæki] **1.** *n.* a thing; a nameless gadget. ♦ *Is this your doowacky? I was going to throw it away.* **2.** *n.* money. ♦ *You got some doowacky I can borrow?*

**dorf** [dorf] *n.* a stupid person; a weird person. ♦ *You are a prize-winning dorf.*

**dork** [dork] **1.** *n.* the penis. (Usually objectionable.) ♦ *Paul told a joke about a dork, but everybody just sat there and looked straight ahead.* **2.** *n.* a jerk; a strange person. (See also **megadork.**) ♦ *Ye gods, Sally! You are a dork!*

**dork off** *in.* to waste time; to goof off. ♦ *The whole class was dorking off and the teacher got furious.*

**dorkus maximus** ['dorkəs 'mæksıməs] *n.* a simpleton or fool; a great fool. ♦ *Tim is now the dorkus maximus of our dorm since he broke the dorm's television set.*

**double six** *n.* a year; a pair of six-month periods. (Streets.) ♦ *Johnny spent a double six in the slammer.*

**double-bagger 1.** *n.* a hit good for two bases in baseball. ♦ *Wilbur hit a nice double-bagger in the top of the fourth.* **2.** *n.* a very ugly person. (Cruel. With a face so ugly that it takes two paper bags to conceal it. See also **Bag your face!**; **brown bag it**; **triple-bagger**; **coyote-ugly**.) ♦ *Fred is what I would call a double-bagger. What a mug!*

**double-dome 1.** *n.* an intellectual. ♦ *It's not that what the double-domes say is wrong, it's that they are so sure that they are right that scares me.* **2.** *mod.* intellectual. ♦ *Most kids need to be exposed to double-dome profs at college for a while.*

**dough head** *n.* a nerd; a simpleton. ♦ *Tom, don't be such a dough head. Read the instructions and do it right.*

**doughboys** *n.* the female breasts. ♦ *What a nice pair of doughboys!*

the **down low** AND the **DL** *n.* the information or explanation; the **lowdown**. (Streets.) ♦ *Give me the haps. What the down low?*

**down with** sth **1.** *mod.* comfortable with something; comfortable. (Usually with *get*.) ♦ *Let's get down with some good music.* **2.** *mod.* ill with something; sick in bed with something. ♦ *I was down with the flu for two weeks.*

**down with the haps** *mod.* knowing what's happening; comfortable with what's happening. (Streets.) ♦ *Tell me what's going on! I gotta be down with the haps.*

**draft board** *n.* a tavern; a saloon. (Alludes to draft beer.) ♦ *Let's stop in the local draft board and toss a couple.*

**drag ass around** *in.* to go around looking very sad and depressed. (Usually objectionable.) ♦ *Why do you drag ass around all the time, Tom?*

**dragged out** *mod.* exhausted; worn-out. ♦ *I feel so dragged out. I think I need some iron.*

**drain the bilge** *tv.* to empty one's stomach; to vomit. ♦ *Fred left quickly to drain the bilge.*

**drain the dragon** *tv.* [for a male] to urinate. ♦ *Bobby? He went to drain the dragon.*

the **drink** *n.* the water of the ocean, lake, pond, etc. ♦ *Stay away from the edge of the boat unless you want to fall in the drink.*

**drinkage** *n.* drinking; drinks. ♦ *The school tried to outlaw drinkage on campus but failed.*

**drinkies** *n.* drinks; liquor. ♦ *Okay, kids, it's drinkies all around.*

**dro** AND **hydro** *n.* hydroponically grown marijuana. ♦ *He raises hydro in his basement.* ♦ *He's got some kickin' dro. Want a piece?*

**droid** [drɔɪd] *n.* a robot-like person; a nerd. (From *android.*) ♦ *Beavis is as close to a droid as we'll ever see.*

**droob** AND **drube** [drub] *n.* a dullard; an oaf. ♦ *Who's the droob standing by the punch bowl?*

**drool-proof** *mod.* can withstand idiots who drool. (Of well-written software that even drooling idiots can operate without crashing.) ♦ *This software package is drool-proof. Even my grandmother could use it.*

**drop a bundle (on** so**)** *tv.* to spend a lot of money pleasing or entertaining someone. ♦ *I dropped a bundle on the candidate, and it didn't help me at all.*

**drop a bundle (on** sth**)** *tv.* to pay a lot of money for something. ♦ *Pete dropped a bundle on this car.*

**drop** so **some knowledge** *tv.* to give someone some information. ♦ *Come on, what's the 411? Drop some knowledge on me.*

**drop-dead list** *n.* an imaginary list of annoying people whom one could live happily without. ♦ *You are right at the top of my drop-dead list.*

**dropped** *mod.* arrested. ♦ *Harry the Horse was dropped only once last year.*

**drugola** [drəgˈolə] *n.* a bribe paid by drug dealers to the police for protection. (Patterned on **payola**.) ♦ *Frank pays a little drugola, but mostly the cops never come into this area anyway.*

**drunk** *n.* [of baseball bases] loaded. ♦ *We're at the bottom of the fifth and the bases are drunk.*

**dub** [dəb] **1.** *tv. & in.* to duplicate something; to copy something. ♦ *Dub this and keep a copy yourself.* **2.** *n.* a duplicate; a copy. ♦ *The dub was so poor we couldn't understand the dialogue.*

**dubage** AND **doobage** [ˈdubɪdʒ] *n.* drugs; marijuana. ♦ *I detect the smell of dubage in the hallway!*

**dub-dub-dub** AND **dubya-dubya-dubya** *n.* double-u, double-u, double-u, the letters WWW found in World Wide Web addresses. (The second version is merely a colloquial pronunciation of double-u, and neither is commonly written or printed.) ♦ *Our address is dub-dub-dub dot reindeer dot com.*

**duck-squeezer** *n.* someone with strong concerns about the environment and conservation, especially rescuing oil-covered ducks. ♦ *Some duck-squeezers were complaining about what the new dam might do.*

**dude (oneself) up** *tv.* to dress in fancy or stylish clothing. ♦ *Why don't you dude yourself up so we can go out tonight?*

**dude up** *in.* to dress up. (Possibly as in *doo-ed up*.) ♦ *Let's get all duded up and go out.*

**dudette** ['dudɛt] *n.* a young woman; the feminine of dude. ♦ *The place was filled with good-looking dudettes, just waiting for the right guy to come along.*

**dudical** ['dudɪkḷ] *mod.* really good. (Derived from dude.) ♦ *It is truly dudical to see you here, Dave.*

**duky** ['duki] *n.* feces. (Originally black and primarily juvenile. Possibly from the juvenile euphemism *duty* = job = bowel movement.) ♦ *Mommy, there's duky in Jimmy's diaper.*

**dullsville** ['dəlzvɪl] **1.** *n.* a dull place. ♦ *This place is just dullsville!* **2.** *n.* something dull. ♦ *When each movie I see turns into dullsville, I want to give up seeing them.*

**dumbshit 1.** *n.* a very stupid person. (Rude and derogatory.) ♦ *He's a dumbshit. He can't do any better than that.* **2.** *mod.* stupid; dumb. (Usually objectionable.) ♦ *That was really a dumbshit thing to do.*

**dumbski** ['dəmski] **1.** *n.* a stupid person. ♦ *He's not the dumbski he seems to be.* **2.** *mod.* stupid; dumb. ♦ *It is not a dumbski idea!*

**Dump it.** *tv.* throw it away. ♦ *We don't need it. Get rid of it! Dump it!*

**durge** *n.* a moron; a jerk. ♦ *You incredible durge! What were you thinking?*

**duster** *n.* the buttocks. (See also rusty-dusty.) ♦ *She fell down right on her duster.*

**dust-up** *n.* a fight. ♦ *There was a dust-up at the party that ruined the evening for everyone.*

**dweeb** [dwib] **1.** *n.* an earnest student. (Collegiate.) ♦ *Don't call Bob a dweeb! Even if he is one.* **2.** *n.* a strange or eccentric person; a nerd. ♦ *This place is filled with dweebs of all sizes.*

**dynamic duo** [daɪ'næmɪk 'duo] *n.* a very special pair of people or things. (From the *Batman* television program. Used mostly for humor.) ♦ *The dynamic duo, Beavis and Fred, showed up late and without the beer.*

**dynamite 1.** *n.* anything potentially powerful: a drug, news, a person. ♦ *The story about the scandal was dynamite and kept selling papers for a month.* **2.** *mod.* excellent; powerful. ♦ *I want some more of your dynamite enchiladas, please.*

# E

**eagle** *n.* a dollar bill. (From the picture of the eagle on the back.) ♦ *This thing ain't worth four eagles!*

**eagle freak** *n.* someone with strong concerns about the environment and conservation, especially the preservation of the eagle. (A play on **eco freak**.) ♦ *The eagle freaks oppose building the dam.*

**ear candy** *n.* soft and pleasant popular music; music that is sweet to the ear. ♦ *I find that kind of ear candy more annoying than heavy metal.*

**ear hustle** *in.* to eavesdrop. ♦ *I was ear hustling while you were talking and felt I had to correct something you said about me.*

**ear-duster** *n.* a gossipy person. ♦ *Sally is sort of an "ear-duster," but she's all heart.*

**early beam(s)** *n.* dawn; early morning. (Streets.) ♦ *He was away every day, early black to early beam.*

**early black** *n.* dusk; early evening. (Streets.) ♦ *He was away every day, early black to early beams.*

**earth pads** *n.* shoes. (Streets.) ♦ *Where are your earth pads, girlfriend? You can't go to town with nekkid feet!*

**Earth to** *so. phr.* Hello *someone*, are you listening? (A means of getting the attention of someone who is

Eat my shorts!

ignoring you or who is daydreaming. As if one were on the earth, trying to contact someone in a spaceship. The implication is that the person being addressed is **spacy**.) ♦ *Earth to Mom! Earth to Mom! What's for dinner?*

**Eat me!** *tv.* an expression meaning roughly *suck my genitals.* (Usually objectionable.) ♦ *Eat me, you creep!*

**Eat my shorts!** *sent.* Leave me alone!; Nonsense!; Drop dead! ♦ *You think I'm going to clean up after you? Eat my shorts!*

**eat** one's **gun** *tv.* to commit suicide by firing one's gun into one's mouth. ♦ *The cop was very depressed and ended up eating his gun.*

**eat** so's **lunch** *tv.* to best someone; to defeat, outwit, or win against someone. (In the way that a school bully takes away children's lunches and eats them at recess.)

♦ *The upstart ABC Computer Company is eating IBM's lunch.*

**eco freak** AND **eco nut** ['iko frik AND 'iko nət] *n.* someone with strong concerns about the environment and conservation. (Mildly derogatory. From *ecology*.) ♦ *They call me an eco freak, which is okay by me.* ♦ *The eco nuts are protesting the tree trimming.*

**eddress** *n.* an electronic address. ♦ *Please tell me your eddress so I can send you some e-mail.*

**effing** AND **F-ing** *mod.* fucking. (Usually objectionable.) ♦ *What an effing stupid idea!* ♦ *Who is that F-ing idiot.*

**egg-beater 1.** *n.* an outboard boat motor. ♦ *My egg-beater has been acting up, so I didn't go out on the lake today.* **2.** *n.* a helicopter. ♦ *The egg-beater landed on the hospital roof.*

**egg-sucker** *n.* a flatterer; a sycophant. ♦ *The guy is a chronic egg-sucker. Ignore him.*

the **eighty-eight** *n.* a piano. (Pianos have eighty-eight keys.) ♦ *Sam can really beat the eighty-eight.*

**electrified** *mod.* alcohol intoxicated. ♦ *Her eyes were staring straight ahead, and I knew she was electrified.*

**elevated** *mod.* alcohol intoxicated; tipsy. ♦ *Sam was elevated from the drinking he did.*

**equalizer** *n.* a gun; a pistol. (Underworld.) ♦ *Rocko carried an equalizer but wouldn't dream of using it.*

**eternity-box** *n.* a coffin. ♦ *When I'm in my eternity-box, then you can have my stereo.*

**euchre** [ˈjukɚ] *tv.* to cheat or deceive someone. ♦ *Those guys'll try to euchre you, so watch out.*

**evened out** *mod.* back to normal; restored to sanity. ♦ *Finally, at about age thirty, you could say that Sam was evened out.*

**evil twin** *n.* an illegal duplicate of an internet sign-in page into which people enter passwords and credit card numbers, thinking they are signing up for the real thing. ♦ *There was an evil twin operating at the coffee shop, and I gave out my credit card number before I knew what was going on.*

**eye candy** *n.* someone or something worth looking at. (Compare to **ear candy**.) ♦ *The dame is just eye candy! Her brain is occupied with hair and nail appointments, and strained to do even that!*

**eyeball to eyeball** *mod.* face to face. ♦ *Let's talk more when we are eyeball to eyeball.*

**eye-popper 1.** *n.* something astonishing. (Alludes to the comical view of eyes bulging outward in surprise or amazement.) ♦ *What an eye-popper of a story!* **2.** *n.* a very good-looking woman or **girl**. ♦ *Isn't that foxy lady an eye-popper?*

# F

**face time** *n.* time spent face to face with someone. (As opposed to over the telephone or by e-mail, etc.) ♦ *I need to have more face time with my children.*

**fack** [fæk] *in.* to state the facts; to tell (someone) the truth. (Streets.) ♦ *Now is the time to start facking. Where were you?*

**fadoodle** [fəˈdudl] *n.* something ridiculous; nonsense. ♦ *Oh, stop your silly fadoodle!*

**fake off** *in.* to waste time; to goof off. ♦ *Hey, you guys, quit faking off! Get to work!*

**fake the funk** *tv.* to pretend to be in the know; to pretend to be *fly*; to fake being stylish. (Black.) ♦ *He's only faking the funk to survive in the hood. He gets an A in every class in school.*

**fall 1.** *in.* to be arrested; to be charged with a crime. (Underworld.) ♦ *I heard that Mooshoo fell. Is that right?* **2.** *n.* one's arrest; being arrested and charged. (Underworld.) ♦ *Who took the fall for the bank job?*

**fall out of bed** *in.* to fall far down, as with the drop in some measurement. ♦ *The temperature really fell out of bed last night! It was twenty-three below!*

**fancy footwork** AND **fast footwork** n. artful maneuvering; fast and clever thinking. ♦ *Ken did a lot of fancy footwork to get out of that one.*

**fanny-bumper** n. an event that draws so many people that they bump into one another. ♦ *There was a typically dull fanny-bumper in the village last night.*

**fanny-dipper** n. a swimmer, as opposed to a surfer. (California.) ♦ *The fanny-dippers are not supposed to go out that far.*

**fart off** in. to waste time; to goof off. (Usually objectionable.) ♦ *Why are you farting off when there's work to be done?*

**fart sack** n. one's bed. (Military. Apparently a place where one can break wind at will. Usually objectionable.) ♦ *Come on! Get out of the fart sack and get moving!*

**fat city 1.** n. a state of wealth and comfort; **easy street.** ♦ *She's living in fat city ever since she inherited her fortune.* **2.** n. fatness (expressed as a place). ♦ *I've had it with fat city. I'm going on a diet.*

**fat skrill** n. lots of money (See also **skrilla.**) ♦ *The car cost some real fat skrill.*

**feather brain** n. a stupid person. (Also a rude term of address.) ♦ *Hey, feather brain. Wake up and get busy!*

**federal diploma** n. a U.S. bank note. ♦ *I could use a few extra of those federal diplomas.*

**federal jug** n. a federal prison. (Underworld.) ♦ *Lefty is fresh and sweet—just out of the federal jug.*

**feel a draft** *tv.* to sense that one is being rejected; to sense that someone is cool toward one, possibly for racial reasons. ♦ *Oh, man, I feel a draft in here. Let's leave.*

**feen for** sth *in.* to desire something habitually; to be a fiend for something. (From *fiend*, meaning addict, as in dope fiend.) ♦ *Billy Bob's feening for some grub.*

**festy** *mod.* nasty. (From *festered.*) ♦ *That scratch is looking sort of festy.*

**fettie** *n.* money. (Streets. Possibly akin to *confetti.*) ♦ *How much fettie you got with you?*

**field grounders** *tv.* to look downward for cigarette or cigar butts. ♦ *Get good grades unless you want to end up flipping burgers and fielding grounders.*

**filch** sth **(from** so/sth**)** *tv.* to grab or steal something from someone. ♦ *Who filched my wallet from me?*

**filling station** *n.* a liquor store. (From an old name for an automobile service station.) ♦ *Please stop at the filling station and get some suds on your way home.*

**fine wolf** *n.* a sexy or desirable man. (Streets.) ♦ *Who is that fine wolf I seen you with last night?*

**finger wave** *n.* the act of giving someone the finger; displaying the middle finger upright as a sign of derision. (The gesture is taboo.) ♦ *The salute turned into a finger wave when the Major turned away.*

**fink (on** so**)** *in.* to inform on someone. ♦ *Rocko never finks on his friends.*

**fish-kiss 1.** *tv. & in.* to kiss (someone) with puckered up lips. (Collegiate.) ♦ *He fish-kissed me, then ran back to* *his car.* **2.** *n.* a kiss made with puckered up lips. (Collegiate.) ♦ *The actor planted a big fish-kiss right on her lips and frightened her.*

**fitshaced** *mod.* drunk. ♦ *He goes out and gets really fitshaced almost every night.*

**flackery** ['flækɚi] *n.* an advertising agency. ♦ *Ted works for a flackery over on Maple Street.*

**flagged** *mod.* arrested. ♦ *Sally was flagged, and she called her fixer to come get her out.*

**flake down** *in.* to go to bed; to go to sleep. ♦ *After I flake down for about three days, I'll tell you about my trip.*

**flamage** ['fleimɪdʒ] *n.* a flame sense 2; a series of flames and their content; writing or participating in a series of flames. ♦ *The moderator has some warnings about all the flamage of late.*

**flame 1.** *in.* to write an excited and angry note in a computer forum or news group. (See also flamage.) ♦ *Stop flaming a minute and try to explain your position calmly.* **2.** *n.* a verbal attack as in sense 1. ♦ *My e-mail is full of flames this morning!* **3.** *in.* to appear obviously homosexual. ♦ *Man, she's flaming today!*

**flamer 1.** *n.* a blatantly obvious homosexual person. (Primarily and originally for males.) ♦ *He tries not to be a flamer, but what can he do?* **2.** *n.* a person who writes excited and angry notes on a computer forum or news group. ♦ *There are too many flamers on this board to make it interesting and entertaining.*

**flame-war** *n.* an angry and excited exchange of notes on a computer forum or news group. ♦ *A flame-war* *erupted on the board last night and a lot of people said some pretty rude things.*

**flash on** sth *in.* to remember something suddenly and vividly. ♦ *I was trying to flash on it, but I couldn't bring it to mind.*

**flat-hatting** *n.* flying an airplane low and recklessly. (As if flying low enough that only people wearing flat hats could escape being struck.) ♦ *Some of the air force pilots were flat-hatting over the desert when one of them crashed.*

**fleabite** *n.* a small chip off something. ♦ *This cup has a little fleabite, but it doesn't really harm its value.*

**flesh-presser** AND **palm-presser** *n.* a politician. ♦ *Being a flesh-presser is risky during flu season.* ♦ *A palm-presser came to our door to ask us what we thought about his issues.*

**fling-wing** *n.* a helicopter. ♦ *The fling-wing from the radio station is hovering over the traffic jam.*

**flip the script** **1.** *tv.* to lie; to change one's story. ♦ *The guy flips the script depending on whose listening.* **2.** *tv.* to reverse positions in a situation; to turn the tables on someone. ♦ *Now he's the one who's in trouble! That's really flipping the script!*

**flipping burgers** *tv.* cooking hamburger patties in a fast food restaurant as an occupation that school dropouts end up doing. (An occupation that offers practically no opportunities for advancement.) ♦ *Do you want to spend the rest of your life flipping burgers! Do your damn homework!*

flipping burgers: "You miss school don't you?"

**float an air biscuit** *tv.* to break wind; to fart. ♦ *Who floated the air biscuit? P.U.*

**fluff** [fləf] **1.** *n.* nonsense; irrelevant stuff; hype. ♦ *Cut out the fluff and talk straight.* **2.** *tv. & in.* to make an error; to do something incorrectly. ♦ *Todd fluffs his lines in the same place every night.*

**flusher** *n.* a toilet. (Compared to an outhouse.) ♦ *I hear they put in a flusher over at the Babbits'.*

**fly light** *in.* to skip a meal or eating. ♦ *Nothing for me, thanks. I'm flying light today.*

**fly mink** *n.* a fine woman; a sexually attractive woman. (Black. See also mink.) ♦ *Who was that fly mink I saw you with last night?*

**foam** *n.* beer. ♦ *All the guy thinks about is foam.*

**FOBlish** *n.* rudimentary English; English spoken by someone who is FOB = fresh off the boat. ♦ *I can't* *understand your FOBlish! Let me speak to your supervisor.*

**fo-fo** *n.* a .44-caliber pistol. (See also **deuce-deuce**.) ♦ *He traded up his deuce-deuce for a fo-fo.*

**foodie** *n.* someone who is interested in foods, cooking, and the latest food and restaurant fads. ♦ *The foodies are all clamoring for fried sweet potatoes with salmon.*

**foozle** ['fuzl] **1.** *n.* an error; a messed up task. ♦ *What a stupid foozle!* **2.** *tv.* to mess something up; to bungle something. ♦ *Who foozled the copying machine?*

**for kicks** *mod.* for fun; for a thrill. ♦ *We just did it for kicks. We didn't mean to hurt anyone.*

**fosho** *mod.* for sure. (Streets.) ♦ *I'll be there on time fosho.*

**four-bagger** *n.* a home run in baseball. ♦ *Wilbur hit his third four-bagger of the season.*

**four-one-one** AND **411** *n.* information; the details about something or someone. (In the U.S., the telephone number of directory assistance or information is 411.) ♦ *What's the 411 on the new guy in the front office?*

**four-topper** *n.* a restaurant table that will seat four people. (Restaurant jargon.) ♦ *Please seat these two couples at the four-topper in the corner.*

**fox** *n.* an attractive girl or young woman. ♦ *Man, who was that fox I saw you with?*

**fox trap** *n.* an automobile customized and fixed up in a way that will attract women. ♦ *I put every cent I earned into my fox trap, but I still repelled women.*

**foxy lady** *n.* a sexually attractive woman or girl. ♦ *A couple of foxy ladies stopped us on the street.*

**frantic** *mod.* great; wild. ♦ *We had a frantic time at Chez Freddy.*

**freak mommy** *n.* a good-looking female. ♦ *Sally is such a freak mommy. My eyes just water!*

**freaker 1.** *n.* an incident that causes someone to **freak (out).** (Collegiate.) ♦ *Wasn't that weird? A real freaker.* **2.** *n.* a **freaked (out)** person. (Collegiate.) ♦ *Some poor freaker sat in the corner and rocked.*

**free show** *n.* a peek at a private part of someone's body, usually a woman. ♦ *Martin looked like the type who was always waiting for a free show that was never to be.*

**freezer burn** *n.* an imaginary reaction to seeing brightly sparkling jewelry, especially diamonds. ♦ *He's really iced out! I got freezer burn just looking at him.*

**fresh and sweet** *mod.* just out of jail. (Streets.) ♦ *Hey, Lefty, you look all fresh and sweet.*

**Frisco** ['frɪsko] *n.* San Francisco, California. (Said to be objected to by residents of that city. Still in use despite the claim.) ♦ *My cousin lives in Frisco.*

**friz** [frɪz] *n.* a Frisbee. ♦ *Whose friz is that in the tree?*

**frog slicing** *n.* biology class; a biology course. (A dysphemism.) ♦ *Dave dreaded going to frog slicing. The smell got to him.*

**from (the) git-go** *mod.* from the very start. (See also **jump (street).**) ♦ *This kind of thing has been a problem from the git-go.*

**front off about** sth *in.* to complain about something; to be brash and resentful about something; to be confrontational about something. ♦ *Todd was fronting off about his assignment and got a detention for it.*

**fronts** *n.* clothing; a sports jacket. ♦ *You got some good-looking fronts there.*

**froody** ['frudi] *mod.* grand; wonderful; cool. (From Douglas Adams's *The Hitchhiker's Guide to the Galaxy*.) ♦ *The curtains parted to the most froody, funky set I've ever seen.*

**frosted (over)** *mod.* angry; annoyed. ♦ *The clerk was really frosted over when I asked for a better one.*

**froth** *n.* a beer. ♦ *How about another pitcher of frost, innkeeper?*

**froyo** *n.* frozen yogurt. ♦ *Let's stop at the store and get some froyo.*

**fuck 1.** *tv. & in.* to copulate [with] someone. (Taboo. Usually objectionable. It should be noted that English does not have a one-word, standard, transitive verb for this act. All expressions with the same meaning are phrases, slang, or colloquial.) ♦ *They want to fuck all night.* **2.** *n.* an act of copulation. (Taboo. Usually objectionable.) ♦ *I need a fuck.* **3.** *n.* a person with whom one can copulate. (Taboo. Usually objectionable.) ♦ *Man, he's a good fuck if I ever saw one.* **4.** *n.* semen. (Taboo. Usually objectionable.) ♦ *Clean up that fuck before somebody sees it!* **5.** *exclam.* an exclamation of anger or exasperation. (Usually **(Oh,) fuck!** Taboo. Usually objectionable.) ♦ *Oh, fuck! I'm outa beer.*

**Fuck a duck!** AND **Fuck a dog!** *exclam.* Oh, hell!, an expression of anger or distress. (Taboo. Usually objectionable.) ♦ *Fuck a duck! I won't do it!* ♦ *Get up at 6:00 A.M.? Fuck a dog!*

**fuck buddy** AND **fuck puppet** *n.* a sexual partner with whom one has no romantic or nonsexual interests. (Usually objectionable.) ♦ *Bob and Barb are just fuck buddies. They really don't care a thing about each other.* ♦ *She showed up about midnight with her cheap fuck puppet in tow.*

**fuck bunny** AND **FB** *n.* someone who just loves to copulate. (Usually a female. Taboo. Usually objectionable.) ♦ *She's a real fuck bunny, isn't she?*

**Fuck it (all)!** *exclam.* Damn! (Taboo. Usually objectionable.) ♦ *Oh, fuck it all! I don't care what you do!*

**Fuck it, shit happens, drive on.** AND **Fuck it, shit happens, move on.; FISHDO; FISHMO** *sent. & comp. abb.* Sorry about your trouble, forget it and get on with your life. (Usually objectionable.) ♦ *Stop going on and on about your problem. FISHMO.* ♦ *Grow up, chum. Fuck it, shit happens, drive on.*

**Fuck it!** *tv.* To hell with it!; Forget it! (Taboo. Usually objectionable.) ♦ *Your idea is stupid. Fuck it! Try something else.*

**fuck nut** *n.* an idiot. (A fucking nutcase. Usually objectionable.) ♦ *Bob is such a fuck nut. If his head wasn't screwed on, he'd leave it at home!*

**fuck puppet** Go to **fuck buddy**.

**fuck** SO **over** *tv.* to give someone a very hard time; to abuse someone physically or mentally; to cheat, deceive, or trick someone. (Taboo. Usually objectionable.) ♦ *The big guys fucked him over for a while and then let him go.*

**fuck** sth **up** *tv.* to mess something up; to wreck something. (Usually objectionable.) ♦ *Who fucked up my file cabinet?*

**fuck with** so *in.* to cause trouble for someone; to threaten someone. (Taboo. Usually objectionable.) ♦ *Don't fuck with me if you know what's good for you!*

**fuckable 1.** *mod.* readily agreeable to copulation. (Taboo. Usually objectionable.) ♦ *About midnight, she got sorta fuckable, and then she fell asleep.* **2.** *mod.* highly desirable for copulation; suitable or acceptable for copulation. (Taboo. Usually objectionable.) ♦ *Isn't he about the most fuckable hunk you've ever seen?*

**fuckathon** *n.* serial copulation or sexual activity; an orgy. (Taboo. Usually objectionable.) ♦ *It was no honeymoon. It was a first-class fuckathon!*

**fuck-brained 1.** *mod.* stupid; mindless. (Taboo. Usually objectionable.) ♦ *What a stupid, fuck-brained idea!* **2.** *mod.* obsessed with sex. (Taboo. Usually objectionable.) ♦ *All he thinks about is dames. He is totally fuck-brained.*

**fucked out 1.** *mod.* exhausted from copulation. (Taboo. Usually objectionable.) ♦ *They went at it until they were both fucked out.* **2.** *mod.* totally exhausted from doing anything. (As exhausted as if one had been copulating excessively. Taboo. Usually objectionable.) ♦ *Some fucked-out dude was lying on the floor, and another was collapsed on the chair.*

**fucked up** *mod.* messed up; confused; ruined. (Taboo. Usually objectionable.) ♦ *This whole project is so fucked up, it'll take months to straighten out.*

**fuckery** AND **fuck-house** *n.* a brothel; a house of prostitution. (Taboo. Usually objectionable.) ♦ *This street is just one fuckery after another.* ♦ *The suspect referred to the brothel as a "fuck-house," if you'll pardon my French.*

**fuckface** *n.* a despised person. (Also a term of address.) ♦ *Look, fuckface! Who the hell do you think you are?*

**fuck-freak** *n.* someone who is obsessed with copulation. (Taboo. Usually objectionable.) ♦ *She is a hot little fuck-freak, and she'll wear out any dude that takes her on.*

**fuckhead** *n.* a stupid and obnoxious person. (Taboo. Usually objectionable.) ♦ *Don't be such a fuckhead! Go back there and stand up for yourself!*

**fucking** *mod.* damnable; lousy; cursed. (Taboo. Usually objectionable.) ♦ *Get that fucking idiot out of here!*

**Fucking A!** *exclam.* absolutely; totally absolutely. (Usually objectionable.) ♦ *Q: Will you be at the concert? A: Fucking A!*

**fucking old person** AND **FOP** *n.* an old person. (Usually objectionable.) ♦ *I know who's slowing traffic up ahead. A FOP, that's who.*

**fuck-me boots** *n.* knee-high women's boots that signal that the wearer is willing to copulate. ♦ *Eveline! You simply can't go to the prom in those fuck-me boots!*

**fuck-shit** *n.* a truly wretched and obnoxious person. (Taboo. Usually objectionable.) ♦ *Get out of here, you slimy fuck-shit!*

**fuck-up 1.** *n.* a mess; a hopeless hodgepodge. (Taboo. Usually objectionable.) ♦ *When you went home yesterday, you left behind a first-class fuck-up. Now you can clean it up.* **2.** *n.* someone who does everything wrong; someone who messes everything up. (Taboo. Usually objectionable.) ♦ *Poor Willie is such a fuck-up. What a mess he has made.*

**fudge** [fədʒ] **1.** *in.* to cheat; to deceive (someone). (Disguise of *fuck*.) ♦ *Bill, you're fudging. Wait till the starting gun fires.* **2.** *n.* nonsense; deception. ♦ *I've heard enough of your fudge. Let's get honest, okay?*

**fugly** ['fəgli] *mod.* fat and ugly; fucking ugly. ♦ *Man, is that dog of yours ever fugly! What or who did it eat?*

**full sesh** ['fʊl 'sɛʃ] *mod.* totally; completely. (California.) ♦ *It was a great game. They went at it full sesh the whole time.*

**funk** [fəŋk] **1.** *n.* a bad odor; a stench. ♦ *What is that ghastly funk in here?* **2.** *n.* tobacco smoke. ♦ *Most of those important decisions are made by party hacks in funk-filled back rooms.* **3.** *n.* a depressed state. ♦ *I've been in such a funk that I can't get my work done.* **4.** *n.* cowardice; terror. ♦ *She suffers this terrible funk whenever she has to give a talk.* **5.** *n.* a kind of blues rock; jazz based on gospel music. ♦ *Man, groove on that funk, would ya?*

**funky** AND **phunky 1.** *mod.* strange; far out. ♦ *I like your funky hat.* **2.** *mod.* basic and simple; earthy. ♦ *I like to be around funky people.* **3.** *mod.* smelly; obnoxious. ♦ *This place is really funky. Open some windows.* **4.** *mod.* unkempt. ♦ *Your hair is sort of funky. Comb it.*

**funky-drunk** *mod.* alcohol intoxicated; stinking drunk.
♦ *The guy is funky-drunk, and I think he's going to be sick.*

**funky-fresh** *mod.* very good. ♦ *Mary is funky-fresh when she works out, but a real slow runner when she's been lazy.*

**fuse box** *n.* the head; the brain. ♦ *I'm afraid she's missing a little something in the fuse box.*

**futz** sth **up** *tv.* to mess something up. ♦ *I don't want to futz up the deal, so I will be quiet.*

**fuzz station** *n.* a police station. ♦ *He had to spend about an hour at the fuzz station, but nothing happened to him.*

**fuzzword** *n.* a confusing term usually meant to obscure meaning. ♦ *The current crop of fuzzwords contains a few that have come back from the twenties.*

# G

**gabmeister** *n.* a talk show host or hostess. ♦ *There are so many of these "gabmeisters" that I can hardly keep them straight.*

**gack** sth *tv.* to steal something. ♦ *He gacked some skates off that little kid.*

**gaffle 1.** *tv.* to steal something. ♦ *Somebody gaffled my bike!* **2.** *tv.* to arrest someone. ♦ *The copper gaffled Fred Monday.*

**gaffled** ['gæf|d] *mod.* arrested. ♦ *Fred got himself gaffled for speeding.*

**game time** *n.* time to go do what has to be done; time to go to work. (From sports.) ♦ *Okay, gang, let's get going. It's game time.*

**gank** sth *tv.* to steal something. ♦ *Who ganked my bike!*

**garbanzos** *n.* a woman's breasts. (Usually objectionable.) ♦ *Look at the splendid garbanzos on that chick!*

**garden tool** *n.* a whore; a hoe. (Contrived word play.) ♦ *She's nothing more than a garden tool.*

**gasbag** *n.* a braggart. ♦ *What's the old gasbag going on about now?*

**gashawk** *n.* an airplane. (A play on *goshawk,* a species of hawk. From the point of view of a bird watcher.) ♦ *All we saw this morning were two sparrows and a gashawk.*

**gas-passer** *n.* a jocular nickname for an anesthetist. (Hospitals.) ♦ *My gosh! The gas-passer charged almost as much as the surgeon.*

**gear 1.** *mod.* excellent. ♦ *This jazz is really gear!* **2.** *n.* an asterisk (*). ♦ *The gear stands for anything you want it to stand for.*

**geekazoid** ['gikəzɔɪd] *n.* a social outcast; a nerd. ♦ *If you weren't such a geekazoid, I'd be surprised at the dumb things you do!*

**geek-chic** ['gik'ʃik] *mod.* stylish or fashionable only for social outcasts. ♦ *Why do you have to buy all this geek-chic stuff? Don't they give it away somewhere?*

**geekdom** *n.* the realm of the hard-studying students or geeks. ♦ *This dorm is not exactly geekdom. Almost all the guys here are on academic probation.*

**gel** [dʒɛl] *in.* to relax and let one's hair down. ♦ *I've got to go home and gel for a while. Things are too stressful just now.*

**gender-bender 1.** *n.* a device that changes electrical plugs or sockets to the opposite gender—male to female, female to male. ♦ *You need what's called a gender-bender to match those plugs.* **2.** *mod.* having to do with something that obscures male/female distinctions. ♦ *Those gender-bender hairstyles can be confusing.*

**george 1.** *tv. & in.* to copulate [with] a woman. (Usually objectionable.) ♦ *He was in the back room georging* *some dame.* **2.** *in.* to defecate. (Usually objectionable.) ♦ *Man, I gotta george!*

**geri** *n.* an old person. (From *geriatric.*) ♦ *Some geri slowed down the cafeteria line to a standstill.*

**GERK** AND **gerk** [gɚk] *n.* an elderly simpleton; an old nerd. (Acronym. From *geriatric* and *jerk.*) ♦ *A couple of "gerks" sat on the park bench, snoozing.*

**get a toehold** *tv.* to work one's way into some association or relationship. ♦ *As soon as I get a toehold in the company, I'll be more relaxed.*

**get an eyeball on** *so/sth tv.* to manage to spot someone or something; to catch sight of someone or something. ♦ *When I finally got an eyeball on the speeding car, it was too far away for me to read the license plate.*

**get behind** *sth in.* to enjoy something, such as a drug or music. (Originally drugs.) ♦ *I'm really getting behind heavy metal.*

**get down 1.** *in.* to lay one's money on the table. (Gambling.) ♦ *Get down, and let's get going!* **2.** *in.* to concentrate; to do something well. ♦ *Come on, Sam, pay attention. Get down and learn this stuff.* **3.** *in.* to copulate. ♦ *All Steve wants to do is get down all the time.* **4.** *in.* to dance. ♦ *Whenever I hear that band, I really want to get down.*

**get face** *tv.* to gain respect; to increase one's status. (The opposite of *lose face.*) ♦ *He's doing his best in life to get face.*

**get in the groove** *in.* to become attuned to something. ♦ *I was uncomfortable at first, but now I'm beginning to get in the groove.*

**get naked** *in.* to enjoy oneself thoroughly; to relax and enjoy oneself. ♦ *Let's all go out and get naked tonight.*

**Get off my bumper! 1.** *exclam.* Stop following my car so closely! ♦ *Don't follow me so close! Get off my bumper!* **2.** *exclam.* Stop monitoring me!; **Get off my back!** ♦ *Look, man. I can take care of myself. Get off my bumper!*

**get off (on** sth**) 1.** *in.* to get pleasure from something; to become sexually aroused by something. ♦ *I don't get off on music anymore.* **2.** *in.* to take a drug and experience a rush. (Drugs.) ♦ *Max likes to get off, but he's got his business to run.* **3.** *in.* to do well on something. ♦ *Wayne is getting off on history, much to everyone's surprise.*

**get off the dime** *in.* [for something or someone] to start moving. (To get off the dime that one stopped on in *stop on a dime.*) ♦ *If this project gets off the dime, we'll be okay.*

**get** one's **knob polished** *tv.* to copulate or otherwise have sex. (Refers to a male. Usually objectionable.) ♦ *Man, if you want to get your knob polished, just let me know. I got girls! I got girls you wouldn't believe!*

**get** one's **lumps** *tv.* to get the result or punishment one deserves. ♦ *If she keeps acting that way, she'll get her lumps.*

**get** one's **nose cold** *tv.* to snort cocaine. (Drugs.) ♦ *Shorty is always ready to get his nose cold.*

**get** one's **ticket punched** *tv.* to die; to be killed. (Literally, to be canceled.) ♦ *Poor Chuck got his ticket punched while he was waiting for a bus.*

**get out of Dodge** *in.* to leave a place. (Refers to Dodge City, Kansas, and a cliché from Western entertainment adventures about this town.) ♦ *Things are looking bad here. It's time to get out of Dodge.*

**get pasted 1.** *mod.* alcohol or drug intoxicated. (From paste.) ♦ *Bart got pasted on beer.* **2.** *mod.* beaten; outscored. ♦ *Our team really got pasted.*

**get some yokes on** *tv.* to build up one's muscles. (Bodybuilding.) ♦ *If I keep working at this, I know I can get some yokes on.*

**get spun** *in.* to get drunk. ♦ *Let's go out and get spun.*

**get straight** AND **get right** *in.* to take a dose of a drug to end drug craving. (Drugs.) ♦ *You'll never get straight if you keep smoking that stuff.* ♦ *I need to get right before anything else.*

**get the nod** *tv.* to be chosen. ♦ *Fred got the nod for class treasurer.*

**get with the program** *in.* follow the rules; do what you are supposed to do. ♦ *Jane just can't seem to get with the program. She has to do everything her way, right or wrong.*

**ghetto** *mod.* super; cool. (Streets.) ♦ *He called the iced out pimp 100 percent ghetto.*

**ghetto bird 1.** *n.* someone who hangs around the [black] neighborhood. ♦ *Sam is just a ghetto bird who has lots of skills but no job.* **2.** *n.* a police helicopter. ♦ *I see the light. Some ghetto bird is headed this way.*

**ghetto booty** *n.* big buttocks on a black woman. ♦ *Look at that ghetto booty on that mama.*

**ghost turd** *n.* a wad of lint, as found under a bed. (Use caution with **turd**.) ♦ *There's a lot of ghost turds under the bed.*

**gibber-gabber** ['dʒɪbɚdʒæbɚ] *n.* nonsense; gossip and chatter. ♦ *There sure is a lot of gibber-gabber coming from your room, Jimmy.*

**giffed** [gɪft] *mod.* alcohol intoxicated. (From TGIF = Thank God it's Friday. Said of people who celebrate the end of the workweek with liquor.) ♦ *He left the tavern pretty giffed.*

**giggle goo** ['gɪgl gu] *n.* liquor. ♦ *Can I pour you a little of that giggle goo?*

**giggling** *n.* going to clubs and bars. ♦ *We spent the whole night giggling, but never got really, totally drunk.*

**gimp** [gɪmp] **1.** *n.* a lame person. (Originally underworld. Rude and derogatory.) ♦ *Lefty tried to mug an old gimp with a cane.* **2.** *in.* to limp about. ♦ *I'll gimp over there as soon as I can. It'll take a while on these crutches.*

**girked** *mod.* intoxicated with heroin. ♦ *He shot himself up and was girked in no time.*

**girl thing** *n.* something that women do; something that appeals to women. ♦ *You wouldn't understand. It's a girl thing.*

**Give me a rest!** *exclam.* Lay off!; That is enough! ♦ *Haven't I told you everything you need to know? Give me a rest.*

**Give me (some) skin!** AND **Give me five!; Slip me five!** *exclam.* Shake my hand! (A request for some form of hand touching in greeting.) ♦ *Hey, man! Give me some skin!* ♦ *Give me five, dude!*

**give** one one's **pounds** *tv.* thumping a buddy with the fist out of respect and brotherhood. ♦ *All his buds gave Willy his pounds.*

**give** so **a dig** *tv.* to insult someone; to say something which will irritate a person. ♦ *Jane gave Bob a dig about his carelessness with money.*

**give** so **the shaft** *tv.* to cheat or deceive someone; to mistreat someone. ♦ *The boss really gave Willy the shaft.*

**give** so **up** *tv.* to betray someone; to turn someone in to the authorities. ♦ *No, I didn't give Mooshoo up!*

**gizzy** ['gɪzi] *n.* marijuana. (Drugs.) ♦ *The cops found a little gizzy in the guy's pocket.*

**glam** *mod.* glamorous. ♦ *Wow! Isn't she glam!*

**Gland Canyon** *n.* the cleavage (between the breasts). (Punning on *Grand Canyon.* See also **Mammary Lane.**) ♦ *I'd like nothing better than being lost in Gland Canyon.*

**gleep** [glip] *n.* a fool; an oaf. ♦ *What a gleep! Does he know what's what?*

**glick** [glɪk] a strange person; a nerd. ♦ *Fred seems to be a classic glick, but he is really an all-right guy.*

**glitzy** ['glɪtsi] *mod.* fashionable; glamorous. ♦ *Some glitzy blonde sang a couple of songs, and then the band played again.*

**glock** *n.* a gun; a revolver. (Generalized from Glock, the name of an Austrian manufacturer of semiautomatic pistols. Generic and inexact in this sense.) ♦ *Sam was* *carrying a glock and threatened to end the argument his own way.*

**glom** [glɑm] **1.** *tv.* to steal something. (Underworld.) ♦ *He gloms just about everything he needs.* **2.** *tv.* to take a look at someone or something. (Underworld.) ♦ *Come over here and glom the view of the bank from this window.* **3.** *tv.* to arrest someone. ♦ *The copper glommed Fred on Tuesday.*

**glommed** [glɑmd] *mod.* arrested. (Underworld.) ♦ *Wilmer got glommed on a speeding charge. I didn't even know he could drive.*

**glutes** *n.* the gluteus maximus muscles. (Bodybuilding.) ♦ *I need to exercise to tighten up my glutes.*

**glutz** [glʌts] *n.* a slut; a woman of low morals. ♦ *I didn't say she is a glutz!*

**go bitchcakes** *in.* to go wild or crazy. (Usually objectionable.) ♦ *All this rude talk just makes me go bitchcakes.*

**go commando** AND **go freeball(ing)** *in.* [for a male] to go about not wearing underpants. (The same as free-ball.) ♦ *Bobby is always going commando. Even when it's cold.*

**go for the fences** *in.* to set extremely high goals and do whatever is needed to meet them. (Alludes to attempting to hit a home run against the fences of a baseball stadium.) ♦ *We are going to go for the fences on this one. Don't hold back on anything.*

**go green on** SO *in.* to turn against someone; to move against someone; to get angry at someone; to rage at someone. ♦ *Don't go green on me! You know I'm your best bud!*

**go home in a box** *in.* to be shipped home dead. ♦ *You had better be careful on this camping trip, or you'll go home in a box.*

**go mental** *in.* go crazy; to act stupid. ♦ *Another day in that history class and I know I will go mental.*

**go off on** SO *in.* to berate someone. ♦ *Don't go off on me! I'm not the cause of your problems!*

**go postal** *in.* to become wild; to go berserk. ♦ *He made me so mad I thought I would go postal.*

**go Rinso** [...'rɪnso] *in.* to fail; to collapse in price. (A play on to go *down the drain. Rinso* is a laundry soap that goes down the drain after it is used. Used in the context of the securities markets or other financial setting.) ♦ *I knew my bank account would go Rinso after last month's bills came in.*

**go the limit** *in.* to do as much as possible; to get as much as possible. ♦ *We'll go the limit. To heck with the cost.*

**go Titanic** *in.* to fail; to sink. (Refers to the sinking of the passenger ship *Titanic.*) ♦ *The whole project went Titanic. We're out of a job.*

**go tits up** *in.* to die; to go to ruin; to fall apart. (A play on go *belly up* which has the same meaning. Refers to an animal like a goldfish that turns belly up when it dies.) ♦ *Her firm went tits up after the stock market crash.*

**go zonkers** *in.* to go slightly crazy. ♦ *I went a little zonkers there for a minute. Sorry.*

**go-by** ['gobaɪ] *n.* an instance of ignoring or passing by (someone). ♦ *I got the go-by from her every time I saw her.*

**gold** *n.* money. ♦ *Do you have enough gold to pay the bill?*

**golden** *mod.* excellent; really cool. ♦ *Look at the guy she is with. He is golden.*

**golf-clap** *n.* a quiet kind of "patting" applause like that made in golf tournaments. (One hand quietly claps against the back of the other hand.) ♦ *The audience sat there throughout. Not even a little golf-clap. I think our act is washed up.*

**gonged** [gɔŋd] *mod.* drug intoxicated. (Drugs. Originally on opium.) ♦ *Mooshoo found himself in the alley, gonged.*

**gonzo** ['gɑnzo] **1.** *n.* a silly or foolish person. ♦ *Some gonzo is on the phone asking for the president of the universe.* **2.** *mod.* crazy. ♦ *Who drew this gonzo picture of me?*

**goob** [gub] **1.** *n.* a pimple. (Short for guber.) ♦ *I have the world's greatest goob right on the end of my nose.* **2.** *n.* a nerd; a simpleton. ♦ *Gary is such a goob. Why can't he do anything right?*

**goober-grease** ['gubɚgris] *n.* peanut butter. ♦ *Pass me some of that goober-grease, will ya?*

**goobrain** ['gubren] *n.* a fool; a stupid person. (Also a rude term of address.) ♦ *Look, goobrain, think about it a while. You'll catch on.*

**Good call!** *exclam.* That was a good decision! ♦ *Good call, Walter! You picked the right company to deal with.*

**good-to-go** *phr.* ready to go; prepared. ♦ *I'm set. We're good-to-go.*

**gooey** AND **GUI** *n.* a graphical user interface. (A type of computer control system that uses an orderly layout on the screen with icons and menus that are controlled by a computer mouse. **Gooey** is slang; *GUI* is a technical acronym.) ♦ *Some of the older programs that lack a gooey require a lot less memory to run.*

**goof-proof 1.** *mod.* foolproof; not subject to misuse. ♦ *This scheme is not goof-proof, but it's pretty sound.* **2.** *tv.* to make something foolproof; to take action to see that something cannot be misused. ♦ *See if you can goof-proof it by Monday evening.*

**goofus** ['gufəs] **1.** *n.* a gadget. ♦ *Where is that little goofus I use to pry open these cans?* **2.** AND **goopus** *n.* a foolish oaf. (Also a term of address.) ♦ *You're just acting like a goopus. Be serious!* ♦ *Hey, goopus! What's up?*

**gook** [guk OR gʊk] **1.** *n.* a slimy substance; a sediment or residue. ♦ *Too much of that gook will ruin your engine.* **2.** *n.* a foolish oaf. ♦ *Wow, Chuck is turning into a real gook!* **3.** *n.* a tramp. ♦ *Give the gook some food and wish him well.* **4.** *n.* a prostitute. ♦ *There are a lot of gooks around here in the center of town.* **5.** *n.* a derogatory nickname for various East Asians. (Crude.) ♦ *Let the gooks fight it out amongst themselves.*

**goombah** ['gumbɑ] *n.* a buddy; a trusted friend. (Also a term of address. Ultimately from Italian.) ♦ *He's my goombah. I can trust him.*

**goon** [gun] **1.** *n.* a stupid person; a fool. ♦ *Todd is a silly goon, but he's a lot of fun at parties.* **2.** *n.* a hooligan; a thug or bodyguard. (Underworld.) ♦ *Call off your goons!*

**gooned** [gund] *mod.* drunk. ♦ *His date was gooned by ten, and he had to take her home.*

**goon-platoon** *n.* a platoon of misfits; a platoon that is noted for its errors. (Military.) ♦ *Well, the goon-platoon's done it again!*

**goophead** ['guphɛd] *n.* an inflamed pimple. (Patterned on *blackhead*.) ♦ *You ought to see the goophead on your nose.*

**goozlum** ['guzləm] *n.* any gummy, sticky substance: syrup, gravy, soup, etc. ♦ *Do you want some of this wonderful goozlum on your ice cream?*

**gopher ball** *n.* a baseball pitch that is hit as a home run. (When it is hit, the batter will *go for* home.) ♦ *The center fielder did a dive over the fence trying to get the gopher ball.*

**gorked (out)** [gorkt…] *mod.* heavily sedated; knocked out. (Hospitals.) ♦ *The guy in 226 is totally gorked out now.*

**gouch off** [gaʊtʃ…] *in.* to pass out under the influence of drugs. (Drugs.) ♦ *After taking the stuff, Gary gouched off.*

**grab some bench** *tv.* go to the bench, during a game. ♦ *The coach told Freddy to go grab some bench.*

**grabbers** *n.* the hands. ♦ *Wash your grubby little grabbers before coming to the table.*

**granny flat** *n.* an apartment built into a garage or house for an elderly parent to live in. ♦ *The garage has a granny flat including all utilities.*

**grape shot** *mod.* alcohol intoxicated; drunk on wine. ♦ *After the reception, Hank found himself a little grape shot.*

**grape smugglers** *n.* tight swimming briefs. (As if the wearer had stuffed some grapes into the crotch in order to smuggle them somewhere.) ♦ *He owned a pair of grape smugglers, but never wore them in public.*

**grave-dancer** *n.* someone who profits from or takes advantage of someone else's misfortune. (From *dance on so's grave*, seemingly in celebration of someone else's misfortune.) ♦ *I don't want to seem like a grave-dancer, but his defeat places me in line for a promotion.*

**gravity check** *n.* a fall as from a surfboard, bike, etc. ♦ *She rounded the turn and had a sudden gravity check, resulting in a scraped elbow.*

**gravycakes** *mod.* fine; super. ♦ *This little car is truly gravycakes.*

**graze** AND **browse** *in.* to eat a bit of everything at parties. ♦ *We will just graze on party snacks rather than eat a full meal.* ♦ *I think I'll just browse here and skip going out to dinner.*

**great divide** *n.* a divorce. ♦ *How did Sam survive the great divide?*

**green apple quickstep** *n.* diarrhea. ♦ *He was stricken with the green apple quickstep on the first day of their vacation.*

**green stamps** *n.* money. (From *S&H Green Stamps* given as an incentive to purchase other goods.) ♦ *How many green stamps does this take?*

**greenie** ['grini] *n.* a Heineken (brand) beer. (It comes in a green bottle.) ♦ *Tom ordered a greenie and had it put on his tab.*

**greldge** [grɛldʒ] **1.** *n.* something nasty or yucky. ♦ *That's not greldge, that's just plain mud.* **2.** *exclam.* Nuts!; Darn! (Usually **Greldge!**) ♦ *Oh, greldge! I'm late!*

**grindage** *n.* food. (From the grinding of teeth.) ♦ *Hear my belly? It's crying for some grindage.*

**gritch** [grɪtʃ] **1.** *in.* to complain. (A blend of *gripe* and *bitch*.) ♦ *Stop gritching all the time.* **2.** *n.* a complainer; a griper. ♦ *You are getting to be such a gritch.*

**grogan** *n.* a bowel movement. ♦ *He's in the john, fighting with a grogan.*

**groggery** ['grɑgəi] *n.* a tavern; a place to buy liquor. ♦ *All the groggeries are closed on Sundays.*

**grok** [grɔk] *tv.* to "drink" in a concept or knowledge and assimilate it; to understand something; to appreciate someone or something; to relate to someone or something. ♦ *I don't quite grok that. Run it by again, would you?*

**gronk** [grɔŋk] **1.** *n.* a nasty substance, such as dirt that collects between the toes. ♦ *I don't want to hear any more at all about your gronk.* **2.** *mod.* worthless. ♦ *I don't care about your old gronk car. I'd rather take the bus.*

**ground-pounder** *n.* an infantry soldier. (Military.) ♦ *If you join the army, it means a lot of your life spent as a ground-pounder.*

**grovel** ['grɑvl] *in.* to fondle or pet. ♦ *They spent the whole time in the backseat groveling.*

**grunge** AND **grunch** [grəndʒ AND grəntʃ] **1.** *n.* any nasty substance; dirt; gunk. ♦ *There's some gritty grunge on the kitchen floor.* **2.** *n.* an ugly or nasty person; a repellent person. ♦ *Some grunch came by and dropped off this strange package for you.*

**gubb** *n.* semen. ♦ *Clean up that gubb before somebody sees it!*

**gubbish** *n.* nonsense; useless information. (Computers. A combination of *garbage* and *rubbish*.) ♦ *I can't make any sense out of this gubbish.*

**guck** [gək] *n.* a thick, sticky substance; **yuck.** ♦ *The doctor painted some nasty guck on my throat and told me not to swallow for a while.*

**gug** [gəg] *n.* a repellent person. ♦ *Rocko is not a gug!*

**gumbyhead** ['gəmbihɛd] *n.* someone who does stupid things like the character Gumby. ♦ *Don't be a gumbyhead. Don't drink and drive.*

**gump** [gəmp] *n.* a fool; an oaf. (Like the rural and not too smart Andy Gump of comic strip fame in the early 1900s, later reinforced by Forrest Gump of movie fame.) ♦ *Don't act like such a gump!*

**gunge** [gəndʒ] *n.* a skin irritation in the groin. (Said of males.) ♦ *The sawbones'll give you something for the gunge.*

**gunner** *n.* an earnest student. (Collegiate.) ♦ *The gunners in my algebra class always get the As.*

**guns** *n.* the biceps; large muscular arms. (See also **pythons.**) ♦ *He lifts weights to build up his guns.*

**guppy** *n.* a gay **yuppy**. ♦ *They called themselves guppies, because they were young and urban and gay.*

**guy thing** *n.* something that appeals to men; something that men do. ♦ *We just do it. We don't know why. It's a guy thing.*

**guzzlery** AND **guzzery** ['gəzləˑi AND 'gəzəˑi] *n.* a bar; a liquor store. ♦ *Sam hit every guzzlery on Maple Street on the way home.*

**gweeb** [gwib] *n.* a studious student. (Collegiate. A variant of **dweeb**.) ♦ *I'm in a physics class full of gweebs.*

**gweebo** ['gwibo] *mod.* feeble; despicable; in the manner of a **gweeb**. ♦ *I'm not gweebo. I'm just eccentric.*

**gym shoe** *n.* a disliked person. ♦ *Who is the gym shoe who comes to class in a sport coat?*

# H

**hack around** *in.* to waste time. ♦ *I wanted to hack around for a year after college, but my finances disagreed.*

**hacked** [hækt] *mod.* worn-out; ready to quit. ♦ *What a day! I'm hacked.*

**hacked (off)** *mod.* angry; annoyed. ♦ *Willy was really hacked off about the accident.*

**hacker 1.** *n.* a taxi driver. ♦ *You wonder how some of these hackers keep their licenses.* **2.** *n.* a sloppy or inefficient computer programmer. ♦ *This program was written by a real hacker. It's a mess, but it works.* **3.** *n.* a generally unsuccessful person. ♦ *Poor Pete is just a hacker. He'll never go any place.* **4.** *n.* someone who breaks into a computer electronically. ♦ *Some hacker broke into our computer!*

**half a bubble off plumb** *phr.* giddy; crazy. ♦ *Tom is just half a bubble off plumb, but he is all heart.*

**half-sprung** *mod.* tipsy; alcohol intoxicated. ♦ *Ted was half-sprung and could hardly stand up.*

**hamburger** *n.* a stupid and worthless person—meat. ♦ *The guy is just hamburger. You can't teach him anything.*

**hamburgers** *n.* shares in the McDonald's corporation. (Securities markets. New York Stock Exchange jargon.) ♦ *I want 400 shares of hamburgers.*

**hammer** *n.* the accelerator of a vehicle. ♦ *She pressed down the hammer, and off they went.*

**hams 1.** *n.* legs; hips. ♦ *Her great hams extended over the sides of the chair.* **2.** *n.* the hamstring muscles. (Bodybuilding.) ♦ *Can you think of any exercises that would be good for my hams?*

**hang (around)** *in.* to loiter; to waste away time doing nothing. ♦ *Don't just hang around. Get busy with something.*

**hang** sth **on** so *tv.* to blame something on someone; to frame someone for something. ♦ *Don't try to hang the blame on me!*

**hang with** so *in.* to hang around with someone. ♦ *I'm going down to the corner and hang with the guys.*

**happy juice** *n.* liquor, beer, and wine. ♦ *A little more happy juice, John?*

**happy pills** *n.* tranquilizers. ♦ *She asked the doctor for some happy pills.*

**happy shop** *n.* a liquor store. ♦ *I need something from the happy shop.*

**haps** *n.* things that are happening; events. (Streets.) ♦ *Come in and tell me the haps.*

**hard coin** *n.* lots of money. (See also **coin**.) ♦ *Old Freddie is earning some hard coin these days.*

**hard off** *n.* a dull and undersexed male. ♦ *Willy is a silly hard off. He seems asleep half the time.*

**hardhat 1.** *n.* a protective helmet worn around construction sites. (Standard English.) ♦ *You'll need a hardhat to come into this area.* **2.** *n.* a construction worker. (Usually derogatory.) ♦ *The hardhats didn't care much for the actress's politics.*

**hard-nosed** *mod.* stern and businesslike; unsympathetic. ♦ *It takes a hard-nosed manager to run a place like this.*

**harsh** *mod.* bad; rude. ♦ *She's a harsh lady and doesn't care how you feel.*

**harsh toke 1.** *n.* an irritating puff of a marijuana cigarette. (Drugs.) ♦ *Wow, that was a harsh toke. Yuck!* **2.** *n.* anything or anyone unpleasant. ♦ *Sally can sure be a harsh toke when she wants.*

**a hat trick** *n.* three successes in a row. (Typically, three hockey goals by one player, and other scoring in threes in other sports. Extended use covers three same or different sexual "scores" by a person in a period of time.) ♦ *Walter pulled a hat trick, and the fans roared.*

**Have a blimp!** *exclam.* Have a good year! (A play on *Goodyear Tire and Rubber Company*, which operates the Goodyear blimp.) ♦ *Have a blimp! See you next summer.*

**Have a good one.** AND **Have a nice one.** *sent.* Have a good morning, afternoon, or evening, as appropriate. (A general formulaic expression used at any time of the day or night.) ♦ *Have a good one, cowboy.* ♦ *See you tomorrow, Todd. Have a nice one.*

**have a shit-fit** *tv.* to have a fit; to throw a temper tantrum. (Usually objectionable.) ♦ *If I'm not home on time, my father'll have a shit-fit.*

**have a skinful** *tv.* [for someone] to contain too much alcohol; to be alcohol intoxicated. (*Have got* can replace *have.*) ♦ *Pete had a skinful and just sat there quietly.*

**have a whale of a time** *tv.* to have an exciting time; to have a big time. ♦ *We had a whale of a time at your party.*

**have game** *in.* to have skill; to have spirit or willingness to get involved in the action. ♦ *Man, I still have game! I can do this!*

**have good vibes** […vɑɪbz] *tv.* to have good feelings (about someone or something). (*Have got* can replace *have.*) ♦ *I've got good vibes about Heidi.*

**have gravy on** one's **grits** *tv.* to be rich. ♦ *He got himself a good job and has gravy on his grits while I'm still eating taters.*

**have** one's **brain on a leash** *tv.* to be drunk. ♦ *Wayne had his brain on a leash before he even got to the party.*

**have shit for brains** *tv.* to be exceedingly stupid. (Usually objectionable.) ♦ *You have shit for brains if you think you can get away with it.*

**have snow on the roof** *phr.* to have white or much gray hair. ♦ *Come on, judge, you've had hair on the roof for years!*

**have sth on the brain** *tv.* to be obsessed with something. (*Have got* can replace *have.*) ♦ *I have money on the brain, I guess.*

**hazel** ['hezl] *n.* heroin. (Drugs. A variety of H.) ♦ *She wants to spend the evening with hazel.*

**headache man** *n.* a male law enforcement agent. ♦ *The headache man was here to see you, Ernie.*

**Headstone City** *n.* a cemetery. ♦ *Our house is just one block after the large Headstone City on the left.*

**heavy artillery** *n.* powerful or persuasive persons or things. ♦ *Finally, the mayor brought out the heavy artillery and quieted things down.*

**heavy bread** AND **heavy money** *n.* a great deal of money. ♦ *Man, that car cost some heavy bread.* ♦ *He can afford it. He pulls down some heavy bread.*

**heavy into** so/sth *mod.* much concerned with someone or something; obsessed with someone or something. ♦ *Freddie was heavy into auto racing and always went to the races.*

**heavy scene** *n.* a serious state of affairs; an emotionally charged situation. ♦ *Man, that meeting was really a heavy scene.*

**heavy soul** *n.* heroin. (Streets.) ♦ *Your heavy soul will be on your back forever.*

**hecka** *mod.* a less intense version of **hella**; heck of a. (Streets.) ♦ *Dude, that's one hecka mess!*

**heinous** *n.* bad; bad-looking; horrible, as in *heinous crime*. (A standard English word, used in a slangy context.) ♦ *Where on earth did you get that heinous outfit?*

**helium head** ['hiliəm 'hɛd] *n.* a fool; an **airhead**. ♦ *Well, what's that helium head done now?*

**hell around** *in.* to go around making trouble or noise. ♦ *Who are those kids who are out there helling around every night?*

**hella** *mod.* (a) hell of (a) (Streets.) ♦ *That's a hella long way to Vegas.*

**hellacious** [hɛl'eʃəs] **1.** *mod.* terrible. ♦ *The heat was hellacious, and the mosquitoes wouldn't leave us alone.* **2.** *mod.* wild; excellent. (Use caution with **hell**.) ♦ *What a hellacious good time we had!*

**Hello?** *exclam.* Did you hear me?; Are you aware that I am talking to you? ♦ A: *I don't want any of that.* B: *Here, have some.* A: *Hello? No, I don't want any.*

**hellpig** *n.* a fat and ugly girl or woman. (Derogatory.) ♦ *Comb your hair. You look like some hellpig!*

**Here's the deal.** *tv.* This is the plan, scheme, or proposition. ♦ *Okay, here's the deal. You pass the ball to Bob, and I'll run in the opposite direction.*

**herped up** *mod.* infected with the *herpes simplex* virus. ♦ *Why do all the boys treat me like I was herped up or something?*

**heteroflexible** *mod.* bisexual. (Contrived. A blend of *heterosexual* + *flexible*.) ♦ *He has preferences, but basically, he's heteroflexible.*

**hiddy** AND **hidi** ['hɪdi] **1.** *mod.* hideous. ♦ *That skirt is just hiddy! Get a life!* **2.** *mod.* hideously drunk; very drunk. ♦ *Fred was totally hidi. He fell asleep under the table.*

**high ups** AND **higher ups** *n.* the people in charge. ♦ *One of the higher ups is coming down to talk to you.*

**high-maintenance** *mod.* [of a person] requiring much care and coddling. ♦ *He's sort of a high-maintenance guy. He requires lots of reassurance.*

**hip-shooter** *n.* someone who talks without thinking; someone who speaks very frankly. ♦ *He's just a loud-mouthed hip-shooter. Pay no attention.*

**hit by the stupid stick** *mod.* made to act really stupid. ♦ *Nobody can be that dumb. You must have been hit by the stupid stick.*

**hit by the ugly stick** *mod.* made to be very ugly. ♦ *She is so lame. Looks like she was hit by the ugly stick till it broke!*

**hit me on the hip** *tv.* call me on my pager. (Pagers are usually worn attached to one's belt or in a pants packet.) ♦ *When you need me, just hit me on the hip.*

**hit on** so *in.* to flirt with someone; to make a pass at someone. ♦ *The women were all hitting on George, but he didn't complain.*

**hit on** sth *in.* to discover something; to think up or invent something. ♦ *She hit on a new scheme for removing the impurities from drinking water.*

**hit under the wing** *mod.* alcohol intoxicated. (In the way that a bird is struck by shot.) ♦ *Sally was a little hit under the wing, but she wasn't bad off at all.*

**ho stro** *n.* a location where prostitutes look for customers, a *whore stroll.* ♦ *What're you doing on this ho stro? It's mine.*

**hobeast** ['ho bist] *n.* a whore beast; a promiscuous woman. ♦ *I try to avoid that hobeast.*

**hock a luggie** ['hɑk ɑ 'lugi] *tv.* to cough up and spit out phlegm. ♦ *Tom suppressed the urge to hock a luggie over the bridge railing.*

**hodad** AND **hodaddy** ['hodæd(i)] **1.** *n.* someone, usually a male, who poses (badly) as a surfer. (California. Possibly a blend of ho = whore and *dad(dy)* = male.) ♦ *Who's that hodaddy with the crumby looking board?* **2.** *n.* an obnoxious person; a repellent person. (California.) ♦ *Ted is a total hodad.*

**ho-jo('s)** ['hodʒo(z)] *n.* a Howard Johnson's restaurant or hotel. (Collegiate. Often with *the.*) ♦ *We're going to meet the others at the ho-jo.*

**Hold everything!** *exclam.* Stop everything! ♦ *Hold everything! I forgot my wallet.*

**Hold it!** *exclam.* Stop right there! ♦ *Hold it! Stop!*

**Hold some, fold some.** *sent.* to hold some of your stocks and sell some. (Securities markets.) ♦ *My best advice right now is to hold some, fold some. There is no real trend to the market.*

**hole** *n.* a despised person; an **asshole**. (Usually objectionable. Also a term of address.) ♦ *Sam is such a hole. He needs human being lessons.*

**holmes** [homz] *n.* one's pal or friend. (A variant of **homes.** Usually a term of address.) ♦ *What do you think about that, holmes?*

**homeboy** AND **homegirl** *n.* a buddy; a pal. (Originally between blacks. Also a term of address. **Homeboy** is for males and **homegirl** is for females.) ♦ *Come on, homeboy. Help out a friend.* ♦ *Tsup, homegirl?*

**homes** AND **homey; homie** *n.* a buddy; a pal. (Originally between blacks. Also a term of address. See also holmes.) ♦ *Me and my homie want to go with you.*

**homeslice** AND **home skillet** *n.* a homeboy; a homegirl. ♦ *Ask my homeslice over there if he wants to go with you.* ♦ *Sure I know Davy. He's my home skillet.*

**honey** ['həni] *n.* beer. ♦ *Let's stop at the happy shop and get some honey.*

**honey fuck** *n.* a gentle and loving act of sexual intercourse. (Taboo. Usually objectionable.) ♦ *I told him I'd prefer a honey fuck to a bunny fuck any day.*

**honk 1.** *n.* a drinking spree; a toot. ♦ *Jed's last honk lasted nearly a week.* **2.** *n.* a white male; a honky. (Black. Not necessarily derogatory.) ♦ *There are mainly honks where I work.* **3.** *in.* to vomit. (Onomatopoetic.) ♦ *I can hear someone in the john honking like mad.* **4.** *tv.* to vomit something. ♦ *He honked up his whole pizza.*

**honkers** *n.* a woman's breasts. (Jocular. See also hooters. Usually objectionable.) ♦ *Look at the honkers on that dame!*

**honking** *mod.* huge. ♦ *She showed up with this great, honking jock who kept eating with his hands!*

**hoo-ah** AND **hoo-rah** *exclam.* Yes! ♦ *Are we ready? Hoo-ah!* ♦ *Hoo-rah, hoo-rah, hoo-rah.*

**hood 1.** *n.* a hoodlum. ♦ *A couple of hoods hassled us on the street.* **2.** *n.* the neighborhood; the ghetto; any neighborhood. ♦ *Back in the hood, Bob's considered an important guy.*

**hood rat** *n.* someone who hangs around the [black] neighborhood. ♦ *Sam's just a wimpy hood rat. He never sees any action.*

**hoodie** *n.* a hooded sweatshirt. ♦ *It's chilly. Better grab a hoodie.*

**hook it** *tv.* to get a ride by hitchhiking. (The hook is the thumb.) ♦ *My car broke down and I had to hook it home.*

**hook** sth **down** *tv.* to swallow something down. ♦ *Hook down one of these cookies and see what you think about them.*

**hoops** *n.* the game of basketball. ♦ *Welcome to another evening of college hoops, brought to you by the Nova Motor Company.*

**hooters** *n.* a woman's breasts. (Jocular. Usually objectionable.) ♦ *Look at the hooters on that dame!*

**hoovering 1.** *n.* an abortion. (From the suction used, referring to the vacuum cleaner.) ♦ *She said she thought a hoovering would make things right.* **2.** *n.* an act of sucking up to someone. ♦ *No more of your hoovering! You are a sycophantic pain in the butt!*

**hopfest** *n.* a beer-drinking party. ♦ *We went to a big hopfest over at Willy's, but it broke up early.*

**horizontal hula** *n.* copulation. (Contrived.) ♦ *She wanted to do some of that horizontal hula.*

**hork 1.** *in.* to vomit. ♦ *God! I think I'm going to hork!* **2.** *in.* to spit. ♦ *Don't you hork on my driveway, you slob!*

**horse cock** *n.* a large sausage. (Usually objectionable. Military.) ♦ *Whack me off a piece of that horse cock, would ya, Clyde?*

**horse hockey 1.** *n.* horse dung. ♦ *You don't see horse hockey in the streets anymore.* **2.** *n.* nonsense. ♦ *I've heard enough of your horse hockey.*

**horses** *n.* horse power, as in an engine. ♦ *How many horses does this thing have?*

**hose so down** *tv.* to kill someone. (Underworld. From the image of spraying someone with bullets.) ♦ *The thugs tried to hose down the witness.*

**hoser 1.** *n.* a good guy or buddy. (Probably the same allusion as *fucker*.) ♦ *Old Fred is a good hoser. He'll help.* **2.** *n.* a cheater or deceiver. ♦ *You dirty lying hoser!* **3.** *n.* a moron; a stupid acting person. (Rude and derogatory.) ♦ *Come here, you hoser. I'll show you how to do it.*

**hot item 1.** *n.* an item that sells well. ♦ *This little thing is a hot item this season.* **2.** *n.* a romantically serious couple. ♦ *Sam and Mary are quite a hot item lately.*

**hot number 1.** *n.* an exciting piece of music. ♦ *Now here's a hot number by the Wanderers.* **2.** *n.* an attractive or sexy girl or woman. ♦ *Who's that hot number I saw you with last night?*

**hot paper** *n.* bad checks; a bad check. (Underworld.) ♦ *That teller can spot hot paper a mile away.*

**hot potato** *n.* a difficult problem. ♦ *I sure don't want to have to deal with that hot potato.*

**hot shit** *n.* a male who thinks he is the greatest person alive; a conceited male. (Probably also used for females. Used with or without *a*. Usually objectionable.) ♦ *The jerk thinks he is real hot shit.*

**hot wire** *tv.* to start a car without a key. (By using a wire to carry current around the ignition switch.) ♦ *Lefty hot wired the car and used it for an hour or two.*

**hottie** *n.* a sexually attractive person. ♦ *He's a real hottie! I wonder if he's taken.*

**house moss** *n.* little blobs of lint. (See also **ghost turd**.) ♦ *There is some house moss under the sofa.*

**house of many doors** *n.* a prison. ♦ *Sam just got out of the house of many doors and is looking for somebody to pull a job with.*

**How ya living?** *interrog.* How are you doing? (The response is **Living large**.) ♦ *How ya living, man?*

**humongous** [hju'mɑŋgəs] *mod.* huge. (See also **mongo**.) ♦ *She lives in a humongous house on the hill.*

**humpy** *mod.* sexually aroused; **horny**. (Usually objectionable.) ♦ *I'm so humpy, I could screw a cow.*

**hundo** *n.* hundred. ♦ *How much? A hundo! Geeesh!*

**hungarian** *mod.* hungry. ♦ *Man, I'm hungarian!*

**hurl 1.** *in.* to empty one's stomach; to vomit. (Like the *throw* in *throw up*.) ♦ *I think I gotta go hurl.* **2.** *n.* vomit. ♦ *There's hurl all over the bathroom floor!*

**hurt 1.** *mod.* very ugly; damaged and ugly. (Streets. Similar to **hurting**.) ♦ *That poor girl is really bad hurt.* **2.** *mod.* drug intoxicated. (Streets.) ♦ *Gert was really hurt and nodding and drooling.*

**hurt for** so/sth *in.* to long after someone or something; to need someone or something. ♦ *I sure am hurting for a nice big steak.*

**hurting 1.** *mod.* very ugly; in pain from ugliness. (Similar to hurt.) ♦ *That dog of yours is something to behold. It's really hurting.* **2.** *mod.* seriously in need of something, such as a dose of drugs. (Drugs.) ♦ *Gert is hurting. She needs something soon.*

**hush-hush** ['hǝʃ'hǝʃ] **1.** *mod.* secret; undercover. ♦ *The matter is so hush-hush I can't talk about it over the phone.* **2.** *mod.* secretly. ♦ *They did it so hush-hush that no one knew for a long time.*

**husky** ['hǝski] *n.* a strong man; a thug. ♦ *A couple of huskies helped me get my car unstuck.*

**hut** *n.* a house. ♦ *I've got to go to my hut and pick up some bills.*

**hype artist** *n.* someone who produces aggressive promotional material for a living. ♦ *She is a hype artist for a public relations firm.*

**hyped (up) 1.** *mod.* excited; stimulated. ♦ *She said she had to get hyped before the tennis match.* **2.** *mod.* contrived; heavily promoted; falsely advertised. ♦ *I just won't pay good money to see these hyped up movies.* **3.** *mod.* drug intoxicated. (Drugs.) ♦ *Here comes another hyped up musician.*

# I

**I am so sure!** *exclam.* I am right! (California.) ♦ *You are way rad! I am so sure!*

**(I) love it!** *exclam.* That is wonderful! ♦ *It's wonderful, Ted. I love it!*

**I smell you.** *sent.* I understand you. ♦ *I smell you. No need to go on and on.*

**ice palace** *n.* a jewelry store. (From ice.) ♦ *What do they sell in that ice palace that you could afford to buy?*

**ice queen** *n.* a cold and haughty woman. ♦ *Britney is not exactly an ice queen, but she comes close.*

**iced out** *mod.* wearing lots of diamonds. ♦ *That dude is really iced out!*

**icicles** ['ɑɪs sɪk|z] *n.* pure cocaine in a crystallized form. (Drugs.) ♦ *Are icicles the same as crack?*

**idea box** *n.* the head; the brain. ♦ *You got a good solution up there in your idea box by any chance?*

**If it ain't broke, fix it till it is.** AND **IIABFITII** *sent. & comp. abb.* Don't leave well enough alone.; Just keep tampering. (A play on If it ain't broke, don't fix it.) ♦ *Does it work too well or something? You must say if it ain't broke, fix it till it is.*

**I'll bite.** *sent.* You want me to ask what or why, so, what or why? ♦ *I'll bite. Why did the chicken cross the road?*

**illin'** ['ɪlən] **1.** *mod.* being ill; being sick. ♦ *She was illin' big time and could not come to class.* **2.** *mod.* ill-behaved. ♦ *You are most illin' and you are bugging me, Kim. Stop it!* **3.** *in.* behaving badly. ♦ *Stop illin' and pay attention.* **4.** *mod.* upset. ♦ *What are you illin' about? Everything is ice.*

**I'm gone.** *sent.* I'm getting ready to leave. ♦ *Well, that's all. I'm gone.*

**I'm there!** *sent.* I will accept your invitation and I will be there. ♦ *If you and Tom are going to get together and watch the game, I'm there!*

**in a blue funk** *mod.* sad; depressed. ♦ *Don't be in a blue funk. Things'll get better.*

**in a lip lock** *mod.* kissing. (Contrived.) ♦ *They were rhapsodizing in a lip lock when we came in.*

**in deep 1.** *mod.* deeply involved (with someone or something). ♦ *Bart is in deep with the mob.* **2.** *mod.* deeply in debt. (Often with *with* or *to*.) ♦ *Sam is in deep with his bookie.*

**in** one's sth **mode** *phr.* behaving in a specified mode. (The *something* can be replaced by *work, sleep, hungry, angry,* etc.) ♦ *Todd is always in his play mode when he should be working.*

**in** so's **face** *mod.* irritating someone. (See also **in-your-face**.) ♦ *I wish that the coach wasn't always in my face about something.*

**in the grip of the grape** *mod.* drunk on wine; drunk. ♦ *Wayne was in the grip of the grape and couldn't talk straight.*

**in the know** *mod.* knowledgeable (about something); having inside knowledge (about something). ♦ *Sure, I'm in the know. But I'm not telling.*

**in the soup** *mod.* in trouble. ♦ *I'm in the soup with the boss.*

**in the tube 1.** *mod.* in the "tube" or arch of a large wave. (Surfing.) ♦ *On a day like today, I want to be out there in the tube.* **2.** *mod.* at risk. ♦ *He's in the tube now, but things should straighten out soon.*

**initiative** *n.* cocaine. (Drugs.) ♦ *Maybe I need some more of that initiative to get me going.*

**ink slinger** *n.* a professional writer; a newspaper reporter. ♦ *The ink slingers have been at the candidates again.*

**intense** *mod.* serious; heavy. ♦ *Oh, wow! Now that's what I call intense!*

**internut** *n.* someone devoted to or addicted to using the internet. ♦ *He sits in front of the screen for hours. A real internut.*

**involuntary dismount** *n.* falling off a bike or motorcycle. ♦ *He impacted a monolith and suffered an involuntary dismount.*

**in-your-face** *mod.* confrontational. ♦ *Fred is just an in-your-face kind of guy. He means no harm.*

**issue** *n.* problem. (In colloquial use, **issue** has virtually replaced the word *problem*. It is even heard in a few idioms such as *Do you have an issue with that?*) ♦ *I had* *an issue with my car this morning. It wouldn't start.* ♦ *You are late again! Do you have an issue with our office hours?*

**(It) works for me.** AND **WFM** *sent. & comp. abb.* It works for me.; This proposal works well enough for me and I see no reason to try anything else. (With stress on *works* and *me.*) ♦ *WFM. YMMV (Your mileage may vary.)*

**It's been.** *phr.* a phrase said on leaving a party or some other gathering. (A shortening of *It's been lovely* or some similar expression.) ♦ *Well, it's been. We really have to go, though.*

**(It's) not my dog.** *phr.* It's not my problem. ♦ *So what! It doesn't matter! Not my dog.*

**(It's) showtime!** *exclam.* (It's) time to start! (Said of beginning anything exciting or challenging.) ♦ *Are you ready for action? Okay. It's showtime!*

**I've been there.** *sent.* I know from experience what you are talking about. ♦ *I've been there. You don't need to spell it out for me.*

**ivory tower** *n.* an imaginary location where aloof academics are said to reside and work. ♦ *Why don't you come out of your ivory tower and see what the world is really like?*

# J

**jackal** *n.* a low and devious person. ♦ *What does that jackal want here?*

**jack-shit 1.** *n.* a stupid and worthless person. (Usually refers to a male. Usually objectionable.) ♦ *What a jack-shit! Not a brain in his head!* **2.** *n.* anything; anything at all. (Always in a negative expression.) ♦ *This whole thing isn't worth jack-shit!*

**jagster** *n.* someone on a drinking spree; a heavy drinker. ♦ *Gary is a typical jagster. Drunk for a week and sober for three.*

**jambled** ['dʒæmb|d] *mod.* alcohol intoxicated. ♦ *Jerry was too jambled to stand up.*

**jampacked** AND **jam-packed** *mod.* full. ♦ *This day has been jampacked with surprises.*

**janky** *n.* messed up; bad; inferior. ♦ *Sorry that my room is so janky.*

**jazzy** ['dʒæzi] *mod.* stimulating; appealing. ♦ *That's a jazzy sweater you got.*

**jel** [dʒɛl] *n.* a stupid person. (Someone who has gelatin where brains ought to be.) ♦ *Oh, Wallace, don't act like such a jel.*

**jerkwater** *mod.* rural; backwoodsy; insignificant. ♦ *I'm from a little jerkwater town in the Midwest.*

**Jesus boots** *n.* sandals. (Use caution with *Jesus* in profane senses.) ♦ *Jesus boots are okay in the summer.*

**jet** *in.* to leave a place rapidly; to go somewhere fast. ♦ *Let's jet. It's late.*

**jiggered 1.** *mod.* damned. ♦ *Well, I'll be jiggered!* **2.** *mod.* alcohol intoxicated. ♦ *Todd was more than just a little jiggered.*

**jillion** ['dʒɪljən] *n.* an enormous, indefinite number. ♦ *I've got a jillion things to tell you.*

**jimmy cap** *n.* a condom. (Streets.) ♦ *You better get a jimmy cap on that.*

**jism** AND **chism; gism; gizzum; jizz; jizzum** *n.* semen. (Usually objectionable.) ♦ *This weird doctor took a sample of my gizzum and put it on a microscope slide.*

**jive turkey** *n.* a stupid person. ♦ *What jive turkey made this mess?*

**Joe Six-pack** *n.* the average guy who sits around drinking beer by the six-pack. ♦ *Joe Six-pack likes that kind of television program.*

**johnson 1.** *n.* a thing. (A general or generic name for an unknown person or thing. See also **jones**.) ♦ *Hand me that little johnson.* **2.** *n.* a penis. (Again, a *thing*. Usually objectionable.) ♦ *Zip up, or your johnson'll get out.*

**joined at the hip** *mod.* closely connected; as thick as thieves. (As Siamese twins are joined.) ♦ *Those two are joined at the hip. They are always together.*

Joe Six-pack

**jollies** *n.* a charge or thrill; a sexual thrill; kick. ♦ *He got his jollies from skin flicks.*

**jollop** [ˈdʒɑləp] *n.* a drink of liquor ♦ *She poured a big jollop into each of the glasses and then drank them one by one.*

**jones 1.** *n.* a thing; a problem. (A generic name for an unknown person or thing.) ♦ *This get-rich-quick jones will land you in the joint, Lefty.* **2.** *n.* a drug habit; drug addiction. (Drugs. See also skag jones.) ♦ *That jones is really riding that guy.* **3.** *n.* a desire for someone or something; a craving. ♦ *He has a real jones for chocolate.* **4.** *tv.* to crave something. ♦ *He's jonesing chocolate pretty bad.*

**jonx** *n.* possessions; belongings. ♦ *I got to get my jonx. Then I'll be right with you.*

**joog** [dʒug] *tv.* to stab someone. (Prisons.) ♦ *Lefty jooged the screw.*

**jork** *n.* a worthless person; a combination jerk and dork. ♦ *What a jork! How stupid can you get?*

**jug wine** *n.* cheap wine that is sold in volume, usually in gallon jugs. ♦ *We're having a little do tomorrow—nothing special. A little jug wine and chips.*

**jump smooth** *in.* to give up illegal activities; to become straight. (Underworld.) ♦ *After a night in the junk tank, I knew I had to jump smooth.*

**jump** so's **bones** *tv.* to copulate [with] someone. ♦ *Just one look and he was ready to jump her bones.*

**jump (street)** *n.* the beginning; the start (of something). (Prisons and streets.) ♦ *Way back at jump street, I spotted you as a troublemaker.*

**jungle mouth** *n.* a case of very bad breath; breath like the rotting jungle floor. ♦ *My husband woke up with jungle mouth, and I could hardly stand to be around him.*

**jungled** *mod.* alcohol intoxicated; affected by jungle juice. ♦ *He was jungled before he came here.*

**junk 1.** *n.* herion; drugs. ♦ *Is Sam still on junk? It will kill him.* **2.** *n.* a Caucasian. (Rude and derogatory.) ♦ *Those cops are junk and they hate my guts.* **3.** AND **the junk.** *n.* the genitals. (See also jonx.) ♦ *Stop itching your junk, you freak.* **3.** *n.* possessions. ♦ *I'll be ready to go as soon as I get my junk together.*

**junk fax** *n.* an unwanted and irritating fax message. ♦ *We got nothing but a whole pile of junk faxes today.*

**just off the boat** *mod.* freshly immigrated and perhaps gullible and naive. ♦ *I'm not just off the boat. I know what's going on.*

# K

**kafooster** [kəˈfustɚ] *n.* nonsense. ♦ *This kafooster about me being a cheater is too much.*

**Keep in touch.** *sent.* Good-bye. (Sometimes a sarcastic way of saying good-bye to someone one doesn't care about.) ♦ *Sorry, we can't use you anymore. Keep in touch.*

**keepage** *n.* stuff that you want to keep. (The opposite of garbage.) ♦ *The stuff in that pile is garbage. This stack is keepage.*

**keg** *n.* a beer belly. ♦ *If you didn't drink so much beer, you wouldn't have such a keg.*

**Kentucky fried** *mod.* alcohol intoxicated. (An elaboration of **fried**. Based on the trade name *Kentucky Fried Chicken*, now known as KFC.) ♦ *Man, is that guy really Kentucky fried!*

**kevork** *tv.* to kill someone. (Based on the name of *Dr. Jack Kevorkian*, the physician who advocates, and has practiced, assisted suicide.) ♦ *This guy looked mean— like he was gonna kevork me.*

**kewl** *mod.* an alternate spelling of *cool.*; excellent, neat, and good. ♦ *Man, this is really kewl, I mean truly phat!*

**kibosh** [ˈkaɪbaʃ OR kəˈbaʃ] **1.** *tv.* to end something; to squelch something. ♦ *Please don't try to kibosh the* *scheme this time.* **2.** *n.* the end; the final blow; the thing that terminates something. (Usually with *the*. See also **put the kibosh on** sth.) ♦ *They thought the kibosh was overdone.*

**kick down with** sth *in.* to give forth with something; to dole out a portion of something. ♦ *Hey, man. Kick down with my share of the brewsters!*

**kick freak** *n.* a nonaddicted drug user. (Drugs.) ♦ *Ernie used to be a kick freak, but all that has changed.*

**kick in the wrist** *n.* a drink of liquor. ♦ *You want another kick in the wrist?*

**kicker** *n.* a clever but stinging remark; a sharp criticism; a zinger. ♦ *I waited for the kicker, and finally it came.*

**kickin'** AND **kicken** *mod.* wild; super; excellent. ♦ *I don't know where you get your clothes, but that jacket's kickin'.*

**kicks** *n.* cleats or shoes; gym shoes. (Collegiate.) ♦ *Don't you dare wear those kicks in here!*

**kilobucks** *n.* a tremendous sum of money. ♦ *How many kilobucks does a set of wheels like that cost?*

**King Grod** [...grɑd] *n.* a very repellent male. (California.) ♦ *You are just King Grod! So gross!*

**kink 1.** *n.* a strange person; a kinky person. ♦ *The guy's a kink. Watch out for him.* **2.** *n.* a sexually deviant person.* ♦ *The kinks congregate two streets over.*

**kipe** *tv.* to steal something. ♦ *The punk kiped a newspaper just for the heck of it.*

**kiper** ['kaɪpɚ] *n.* a thief; someone who steals. ♦ *The punk is a two-bit kiper and needs to be taught a lesson.*

**kitsch** [kɪtʃ] *n.* any form of entertainment—movies, books, plays—with enormous popular appeal. ♦ *This kitsch sells like mad in the big city.*

**kludge** AND **kluge** [kludʒ OR klud] **1.** *n.* a patch or a fix in a computer program or circuit. ♦ *This is a messy kludge, but it will do the job.* **2.** *tv.* to patch or fix a computer program circuit. ♦ *I only have time to kludge this problem.*

**kludgy** [ˈklʌdʒi OR ˈklud] *mod.* having to do with an inefficient or sloppily written computer program. ♦ *I don't care if it's kludgy. Does it work?*

**klutzy** [ˈklʌtsi] *mod.* foolish; stupid. ♦ *That was really a klutzy thing to do.*

**knee-deep navy** *n.* the U.S. Coast Guard. (Jocular and derogatory.) ♦ *Join the knee-deep navy and see the beach!*

**knee-mail** *n.* prayer. (A message delivered on one's knees.) ♦ *You'd better be sending some knee-mail on this problem.*

**knock** so **some skin** *tv.* to shake hands with someone. ♦ *Hey, man, knock me some skin!*

**knock** sth **back** *tv.* to drink down a drink of something, especially something alcoholic. ♦ *John knocked back two beers in ten minutes.*

**knock** sth **down 1.** *tv.* to drink a portion of liquor. ♦ *He knocked down a bottle of beer and called for another.* **2.** *tv.* to earn a certain amount of money. ♦ *She must knock down about twenty thou a year.*

**knock** sth **off 1.** *tv.* to manufacture or make something, especially in haste. ♦ *I'll see if I can knock another one* *off before lunch.* **2.** *tv.* to lower the price of something; to knock off some dollars or cents from the price of something. ♦ *The store manager knocked 30 percent off the price of the coat.*

**knothead** *n.* a stupid person. ♦ *Don't be such a knothead!*

**know the score** *tv.* to know the way things work in the hard, cruel world. ♦ *Don't try to con me. I know the score.*

**know where it's at** *tv.* to know the way things really are. ♦ *I know where it's at. I don't need to be told.*

**knowledge-box** *n.* the head. ♦ *Now, I want to get this into your knowledge-box once and for all.*

**knuckle bones** *n.* dice. ♦ *Roll them knuckle bones and tell me that your expense needs earth pads.*

**knuckle sandwich** *n.* a blow struck in the teeth or mouth. ♦ *How would you like a knuckle sandwich?*

**knuckle-dragger** *n.* a strong and stupid man. (Like an ape.) ♦ *Call off your knuckle-draggers. I'll pay you whatever you want.*

**kookish** ['kukɪʃ] *mod.* strange; eccentric. ♦ *Who is the kookish one over there with the purple shades?*

**krudzu** *n.* creeping stupidity. (A play on *kudzu*, an invasive, creeping vine.) ♦ *Your brain is overcome with krudzu. You're getting dumber and dumber.*

# L

**label mate** *n.* someone who records on the same label (as the speaker). (Record industry.) ♦ *Frank Duke is my label mate, and we like to get together and gossip about the record industry.*

**labonza** [ləˈbɑnzə] **1.** *n.* the buttocks. ♦ *Good grief, what a gross labonza!* **2.** *n.* the pit of the stomach. ♦ *That kind of beautiful singing really gets you right in the labonza.* **3.** *n.* the belly. ♦ *I feel the effects of last night's celebration in my wallet and in my labonza.*

**lacy** *mod.* feminine; effeminate. ♦ *The hotel lobby is a little lacy, but it's clean.*

**lame** AND **laine; lane 1.** *mod.* inept; inadequate; undesirable. ♦ *That guy's so lame, it's pitiful.* **2.** *n.* a **square** person. (Streets. Underworld.) ♦ *Let's see if that lame over there has anything we want in his pockets.* **3.** *n.* an inept person. ♦ *The guy turned out to be a lame, and we had to fire him.*

**lamp** *tv.* to look at someone or something. (The "lamps" are the eyes.) ♦ *Here, lamp this tire for a minute. It's low, isn't it?*

**lamps** *n.* the eyes. (Crude.) ♦ *His lamps are closed. He's asleep or dead.*

**landowner** ['lændonəʴ] *n.* a corpse; a dead person. ♦ *Now old Mr. Carlson was a landowner for real.*

**lard** *n.* the police. (Streets. Derogatory.) ♦ *If the lard catches you violating your parole, you're through.*

**lard ass 1.** *n.* someone with very fat buttocks. (Rude and derogatory. See also **crisco**.) ♦ *Here comes that lard ass again.* **2.** *n.* very large buttocks. (Rude and derogatory.) ♦ *I'm gonna have to do something about this lard ass of mine.*

**last roundup** *n.* death. (Western.) ♦ *To everyone's surprise, he clutched the wound and faced the last roundup with a smile.*

**Laters.** *phr.* Good-bye.; See you later. ♦ *See you, Fred. Laters, Henry.*

**lats** [læts] *n.* the *latissimus dorsi;* the muscles of the back. (Bodybuilding.) ♦ *Your lats are coming along fine. Now let's start working on your delts.*

**laugh at the carpet** *in.* to vomit; to vomit on a carpet. ♦ *Tom bent over and laughed at the carpet, much to the embarrassment of the entire group.*

**launch (one's lunch)** *tv. & in.* to empty one's stomach; to vomit. ♦ *When I saw that mess, I almost launched my lunch.*

**lay** so **out in lavender** *tv.* to scold or rebuke someone severely. ♦ *She really laid him out in lavender for that.*

**lead poisoning** *n.* death caused by being shot with a lead bullet. (Underworld.) ♦ *He pifted because of a case of lead poisoning.*

**leadfoot** *n.* a speeder in an automobile. ♦ *There is a lead-foot driving behind me and wanting to pass.*

**lean and mean** *mod.* capable and ready for hard, efficient work. ♦ *Ron got himself lean and mean and is ready to play in Saturday's game.*

**leather or feather** *n.* a choice of beef or chicken for a meal on an airplane. (Contrived.) ♦ *What do the victims get today? Oh, yes, it's leather or feather.*

**leeky store** ['liki stor] *n.* a liquor store. (Black. From *liquor*.) ♦ *Get me some grapes at the leeky store.*

**leerics** ['lırıks] *n.* sexually suggestive song lyrics. (From *leer*. Contrived.) ♦ *For those of you out there who go in for leerics, listen carefully to this tune.*

**leetspeak** AND **hakspeak** *n.* a way of writing or typing on the internet where letters are replaced by numbers or other symbols. (From *elite speak*.) ♦ *The word is spelled p1$t01, rather than pistol in "leetspeak."*

**Let's bump this place!** *tv.* Let's get out of this place! Let's leave! ♦ *Time to go. Let's bump this place!*

**level the locks** AND **level** one's **locks** *tv.* to comb one's hair. (Streets.) ♦ *Just give me a minute to level my locks.*

**Lex** *n.* a Lexus automobile. ♦ *This dude's Lex ain't no ghetto sled.*

**liberate** *tv.* to steal something. (Originally military.) ♦ *We liberated a few reams of paper and a box of pens.*

**licorice pizza** *n.* a 33.3 (speed) vinyl record. (Contrived.) ♦ *Why don't you replace all these silly licorice pizzas with real CDs?*

**licorice stick** ['lɪkrɪʃ stɪk] *n.* a clarinet. (Jazz musicians.) ♦ *Man, can he play the licorice stick.*

**like death warmed over** *mod.* horrible; deathlike. ♦ *A tall, black-garbed gentleman lay there, looking like death warmed over.*

**Like I care.** *phr.* You are telling me this news like it matters to me. (Nonchalant and sarcastic.) ♦ *So, there's problems in South America. Like I care.*

**Like I really give a shit!** AND **LIRGAS** *exclam. & comp. abb.* I really don't care. (Usually objectionable.) ♦ *You are telling me this why? LIRGAS!*

**limpdick** *n.* a weak or ineffective male. ♦ *Stand up for yourself. Don't be such a limpdick.*

**line 1.** *n.* a story or argument; a story intended to seduce someone. (See also **lines**.) ♦ *Don't feed me that line. Do you think I was born yesterday?* **2.** AND **rail** *n.* a dose of finely cut cocaine arranged in a line, ready for insufflation or snorting. ♦ *Let's you and me go do some lines, okay?* ♦ *The addict usually "snorts" one or two of these "rails" with some sort of a tube.*

**lines** *n.* words; conversation. (See also **line**.) ♦ *We tossed some lines back and forth for a while and then split.*

**linkrot** *n.* the gradual fading away of URL links in a web page. (The URLs are replaced by newer addresses or simply are deleted.) ♦ *After a month or two, linkrot sets in and your links become deadends, one by one.*

**lip gloss** *n.* lies; deception; exaggeration; BS. (From the name of a lipstick-like cosmetic.) ♦ *Everything he says is just lip gloss. He is a liar at heart.*

**little boy blue** *n.* a (male) police officer. ♦ *Little boy blue is coming this way, and he's mad.*

**liveware** ['laɪvwɛr] *n.* the human component of computer use. (Patterned on *software* and *hardware*.) ♦ *If I don't get some sleep, you're going to see a liveware crash.*

**living chilly** *in.* living well with lots of diamonds. (Refers to ice, diamonds.) ♦ *That dude's livin' chilly, fo shizzle. He's so iced out!*

**Living large.** *phr.* Doing okay. (The response to **How ya living?**) ♦ *I'm living large. How you doing?*

**log** *in.* to defecate. (See also **dog-log**.) ♦ *Bubba's in the crapper, logging.*

**long bread** AND **long green** *n.* money; much money. ♦ *Man, that must have cost you some long bread!* ♦ *How much long green I gotta lay down for that car?*

**long dozen** *n.* thirteen; a baker's dozen. ♦ *They used to give you a long dozen in that bakery.*

**Lord love a duck!** *exclam.* Wow! ♦ *Lord love a duck, I'm tired!*

**loser** ['luzɚ] *n.* an inept person; an undesirable or annoying person; a social failure. ♦ *Those guys are all losers. They'll never amount to anything.*

**lost in the sauce** *mod.* alcohol intoxicated and bewildered. ♦ *Sally got lost in the sauce at the party and made quite a spectacle of herself.*

**lost-and-found badge** *n.* a military identification tag; a military dog tag. (From the Persian Gulf War.) ♦ *My father still keeps his lost-and-found badge from the Korean War.*

**love bombs** *n.* affirmations of affection. ♦ *These two were dropping love bombs on each other, even though they hate each other's guts.*

**(love) handles** *n.* rolls of fat around the waist that can be held on to during lovemaking. ♦ *Ted worked out daily, trying to get rid of his love handles.*

**low five** *n.* the slapping of hands at waist level as a greeting. ♦ *The two eight-year-olds tried to give each other a low five, but they both hurt their hands.*

**low rent 1.** *n.* a low person; someone without grace or spirit. (Also a rude term of address.) ♦ *Look, low rent, where is what you owe me?* **2.** *mod.* cheap; unfashionable. ♦ *This place is strictly low rent.*

**lowdown 1.** *mod.* rotten; bad. ♦ *What a dirty, lowdown thing to do.* **2.** *n.* the facts on something; the **scuttlebutt** about something. ♦ *What's the lowdown on that funny statue in the park?*

**low-life 1.** *n.* a low person; a repellent person. ♦ *This low-life smells like bacon.* **2.** *mod.* mean; belligerent. ♦ *We don't need any low-life characters around here.*

**low-res** AND **lo-res** ['lo'rɛz] *mod.* poor; unpleasant. (From *low resolution* in a computer terminal. Compare this with **high-res**.) ♦ *The party is lo-res. Let's cruise.*

**lube** *n.* butter. ♦ *Pass the lube, will ya, huh?*

**lucci** *n.* money. (Possibly from *lucre*, "money, reward" as in **filthy lucre**.) ♦ *Can you loan me some of that lucci?*

**luck out** *in.* to be fortunate; to strike it lucky. ♦ *I really lucked out when I ordered the duck. It's excellent.*

**lump** *n.* a stupid clod of a person. ♦ *I am not a lump! I am just sedate and pensive.*

**lumpus** ['ləmpəs] *n.* a stupid oaf. ♦ *Is this lumpus giving you any trouble, ma'am?*

**lunching** *mod.* absentminded; giddy; out to lunch. ♦ *What a giddy twit. He's so lunching!*

**lung-butter** *n.* vomit. ♦ *God, you got lung-butter on my shoe!*

**lurk** *in.* to read computer newsgroups or forums without ever making a comment. ♦ *I've been lurking for a few weeks but just have to get in a few comments.*

**lurker** *n.* someone who reads the messages in an Internet news group or forum without out responding or participating. (Sometimes considered derogatory.) ♦ *These lurkers read everything but never contribute.*

# M

**mace** so's **face** [mes...] *tv.* to do something drastic to someone, such as spraying mace in the face. (Chemical Mace is a brand of tear gas sold in pressurized cans for personal protection.) ♦ *I look at him, and suddenly I just want to mace his face or something.*

**mad money** *n.* money to be spent in a frivolous fashion. ♦ *This is my mad money, and I'll do with it as I please.*

**maggot 1.** *n.* a cigarette. (Probably a play on **faggot**.) ♦ *Can I bum a maggot off of you?* **2.** *n.* a low and wretched person; a vile person. ♦ *You maggot! Take your hands off me!*

**maggot(t)y** *mod.* alcohol intoxicated; very drunk. (A play on **rotten.**) ♦ *Rotten, hell. They were absolutely maggotty!*

**mail** *n.* money. ♦ *The bills are due. I need some mail.*

**major** *mod.* excellent; serious; severe. (Collegiate.) ♦ *This rally is, like, major!* ♦ *Nick is a major dweeb.*

**majorly** *mod.* very. ♦ *He got majorly toasted and ended up staying in the park all night.*

**Make a lap!** *exclam.* to sit down. ♦ *Hey, make a lap and get out of the way!*

**make a mountain** AND **pitch a tent** *n.* to have a morning erection that raises the covers; to have an erection that makes a bulge in one's clothing; to get an erection. ♦ *Bobby makes a mountain almost every morning.* ♦ *When I was in the hospital, I was afraid I would pitch a tent in the morning.*

**make drain babies** *n.* to masturbate (male). (The genetic material goes down the drain. Clever but contrived.) ♦ *My social life stinks. I'm limited to making drain babies.*

**make** one's **bed** *tv.* to be the cause of one's own misery. ♦ *Well, I guess I made my own bed. Now I have to lie in it.*

**make** oneself **scarce** *tv.* to leave; to be in a place less frequently; to be less in evidence. ♦ *Here come the boys in blue. I'd better make myself scarce.*

**make waves** *tv.* to cause difficulty. (Often in the negative.) ♦ *If you make waves too much around here, you won't last long.*

**male blindness** *n.* the imagined failure on the part of a male to see approaching dangers owing to the male's eyes being focused on some well-proportioned female attribute. ♦ *After an attack of male blindness, he walked into a lamppost.*

**mallet** *n.* a police officer. ♦ *Sam was struck by a mallet this noon.*

**malware** AND **evilware** *n.* malicious software; software that intentionally harms normal computer software. (Includes viruses, **spyware**, data miners, trojan horses, and other programs designed to damage or destroy a computer.) ♦ *The industry is concerned about the increase in "malware" but leaders don't know what to do* *at this point. ♦ I used all sorts of stuff to get rid of the evilware, but it's still there somewhere.*

**Mammary Lane** *n.* cleavage. (See also **Gland Canyon.**) ♦ *Let your fingers do the walking down Mammary Lane.*

**manhood** *n.* penis. ♦ *His reflexes automatically protect his manhood.*

**marinate** *n.* to wait calmly for something to happen. ♦ *I'll just sit here and marinate until you figure out what you want us to do.*

**marksman** *n.* a serious college student who works hard to get good marks (grades). ♦ *Bill kept saying that Todd was a geek and a marksman, until Todd flunked algebra.*

**marvy** *mod.* marvelous. ♦ *It's just grand! Marvy!*

**massive** *mod.* excellent. (California.) ♦ *That was a totally massive party, Tiff.*

**massively** *mod.* excellently; totally. ♦ *Max showed up for the meeting massively stoned and singing at the top of his lungs.*

**mattress mambo** *n.* an act of copulation. (Contrived.) ♦ *I get my exercise doing the mattress mambo.*

**maw** [mɔ] *tv. & in.* to kiss and pet; to smooch. (Probably from *maul.*) ♦ *Come on, don't maw me. You've been watching too many movies—or too few.* ♦ *Let's go out somewhere and maw.*

**McD's** AND **McDuck's** *n.* McDonald's, the franchised fast-food restaurant. (Teens and collegiate. The *duck* is a play on the Walt Disney character *Donald Duck.*) ♦ *Can you take McD's tonight, or do you want some slow food?*

**meadow muffin** *n.* a mass of cow dung. ♦ *Jill stepped in a meadow muffin while she was bird-watching.*

**meat wagon** *n.* an ambulance. ♦ *The meat wagon showed up just as they were pulling what was left of Marty out of what was left of her car.*

**meat whistle** *n.* the penis. ♦ *Stop scratching your meat whistle.*

**meatloaf** *n.* unwelcome e-mail messages, jokes, etc., "homemade spam." ♦ *My so-called friends filled up my mailbox with meatloaf while I was gone.*

**meet** *n.* a meeting or an appointment. (Mostly underworld.) ♦ *If this meet works out, we could score a cool million.*

**mega** ['mɛgə] *mod.* large; serious. ♦ *Some mega beast boogied down to the front of the auditorium and started screaming.*

**megabitch** *n.* a truly obnoxious bitch. ♦ *Anne called herself a megabitch and said she didn't care what people thought of her.*

**megadork** ['mɛgədork] *n.* a very stupid person. (See also dork.) ♦ *Tiffany, you are, like, such a megadork!*

**melons** *n.* large breasts. (Usually objectionable.) ♦ *Look at the melons on that babe!*

**mental 1.** *mod.* mentally retarded. (Usually objectionable. Derogatory.) ♦ *The girl's mental. Leave her alone.* **2.** *n.* a mentally retarded person. (Usually objectionable. Derogatory.) ♦ *He's a mental. He'll need some help.* **3.** *n.* a stupid person. ♦ *You're such a mental lately.*

**mental giant** *n.* a genius. ♦ *I'm no mental giant, but I do know trouble when I see it.*

**mental midget** *n.* a stupid person. ♦ *I hate to seem like a mental midget, but what's so great about that?*

**mesh** *n.* a crosshatch or octothorpe, #. (See also pigpen.) ♦ *What does the mesh stand for in this equation?*

**metric shitload** *n.* a whole lot (of something). (Usually objectionable.) ♦ *He is one metric shitload of trouble.*

**mickey mouse ears** *n.* the two lights found on top of a police car. (This is the older form of emergency lights. A bar of lights with varying functions is now the norm in towns and cities.) ♦ *There were no mickey mouse ears, but the jerk inside looked like your average ossifer.*

**miffed** *mod.* angry. ♦ *She was a little miffed when I failed to show up, but she calmed down after a while.*

**milk a duck** *tv.* to do [or not do] something totally impossible. ♦ *She can't do that. That's harder than milking a duck.*

**mingy** ['mɪndʒi] *mod.* mean and stingy. ♦ *Why can't you borrow it? I'm just mingy, that's all.*

**mink** *n.* a woman. (Black.) ♦ *Take this home to your mink. She'll like it.*

**moby** ['mobi] **1.** *mod.* enormous; unwieldy. (Like Herman Melville's great white whale, *Moby Dick*.) ♦ *This is a very moby old car.* **2.** *n.* a megabyte, a measurement of computer memory size. (A megabyte is whale-sized compared to a kilobyte.) ♦ *My fixed disks give me a capacity of over two thousand mobies.*

**modulate** *n.* to relax; to chill. ♦ *Cool it, man. Modulate. Relax.*

**mojo** ['modʒo] **1.** *n.* magic or spells. (Assumed to originate with African slaves. Very old.) ♦ *The old lady was said to possess powerful "mojo" which the others feared her for.* **2.** *n.* power; charisma. ♦ *She seemed to radiate a penetrating mojo that made her easy to deal with.* **3.** *n.* sex appeal; sex drive. ♦ *Man, does he have mojo to spare!* **4.** *n.* heroin; morphine; cannabis. (Drugs. See also on the mojo.) ♦ *Why don't you try to kick the mojo?* **5.** *n.* a narcotics addict. (Drugs.) ♦ *These mojos will rob you blind if you don't keep an eye on them.*

**moldy fig** *n.* an old-fashioned person; a square. ♦ *Don't be a moldy fig! Lighten up!*

**mondo** ['mando] *mod.* totally; very much. (California.) ♦ *This place is like, so, like, mondo beige.*

**mondo bizarro** *mod.* very weird. ♦ *You are one mondo bizarro dude!*

**monet** *mod.* good-looking from a distance. (From the works of the painter, Monet.) ♦ *He's sort of monet. Okay from a distance, but up close: yuck. But that's just my impression.*

**mongo** *mod.* great; very; huge. (Probably akin to humongous.) ♦ *When I get some cash, I'm gonna buy me one mongo car with leather seats.*

**monkey swill** *n.* inferior liquor; strong liquor. ♦ *Where did you get this monkey swill? This would kill a monkey anyway.*

**monolithic** [mɑnəˈlɪθɪk] *mod.* heavily drug intoxicated. (Drugs. A play on **stoned**.) ♦ *She's not just stoned, she's monolithic!*

**moonlit** *mod.* alcohol intoxicated, with **moonshine**. ♦ *He's on the jug again. See, he's all moonlit.*

**moonrock** *n.* a form of **crack** that contains heroin. ♦ *Max was caught with a supply of moonrock on him.*

**mope** [mop] **1.** *n.* a tired and ineffectual person. ♦ *I can't afford to pay mopes around here. Get to work or get out!* **2.** AND **mope around** *in.* to move around slowly and sadly. ♦ *He just mopes around all day and won't eat anything.* ♦ *Stop moping and get moving.*

**mos def** *mod.* most definitely. ♦ *Am I mad. Mos def!*

**motor** *in.* to depart. ♦ *Well, let's motor, you guys. It's getting late.*

**motorized rice** *n.* maggots. ♦ *This dead squirrel stinks and it's alive with motorized rice!*

**mouse potato** *n.* someone who spends a great amount of time using a computer. ♦ *Ever since we got the new computer, Jane has turned into a regular mouse potato.*

**mouth-breather** *n.* a stupid-acting person. ♦ *I always end up with a mouth-breather on a blind date.*

**move on** so *in.* to attempt to pick up someone; to attempt to seduce someone. (Collegiate.) ♦ *Don't try to move on my date, old chum.*

**mud duck** *n.* an ugly person. ♦ *She's a mud duck, but she's got a sense of humor.*

musclehead

**muggle** *n.* someone ignorant about computers, programming, or hacking. (From the name for nonsorcerers in the Harry Potter series of books.) ♦ *This software is great for muggles. It's also drool-proof.*

**munchkin** ['məntʃkən] *n.* a small or insignificant person. ♦ *You're not going to let that munchkin push you around, are you?*

**mungy** ['məŋi] **1.** *mod.* gloppy; messy. ♦ *The spaghetti was cold and mungy by the time it was served.* **2.** *mod.* having to do with an oily feeling of the face of a person who has taken **LSD**. (Drugs.) ♦ *I feel so mungy after I take the stuff. Yuck!*

**musclehead** *n.* a stupid man; a man who has muscle where there should be brains. (Also a rude term of address.) ♦ *Look, musclehead, do exactly what I tell you!*

**musical beds** *n.* acts of sexual promiscuity; sleeping with many people. (From the name of the game *musi-*

cal chairs.) ♦ *Mary has been playing musical beds for about a year.*

**mutant** *n.* a total jerk; a social outcast. (Also a term of address.) ♦ *Sam, you act like such a mutant!*

**My bad.** *phr.* It's my fault and I'm sorry. ♦ *My bad. It won't happen again.*

**my dog** AND **my dawg; my dogg** *n.* my friend; my "pet" and companion. ♦ *Jane's my dawg. We cruise together.*

**my tenda** *n.* my sweetheart; my lover. (Streets. *My tender one.*) ♦ *Come here, my tenda. I want some kissing.*

**mystic biscuit** *n.* a chunk of peyote cactus. (Drugs.) ♦ *Willy thought he got a piece of mystic biscuit, but it was just a moldy raisin.*

# N

**nads** *n.* the testicles. (From *gonads*.) ♦ *He got hit in the nads in the football game.*

**nail Jell-O to the wall** AND **nail Jell-O to a cross; nail Jell-O to a tree** *phr.* to do something that is totally futile. (*Jell-O is a protected trade name.*) ♦ *You're wasting your time. Trying to get him to do that is like nailing Jell-O to the wall.*

the **name of the game** *n.* the way things are; the way things can be expected to be. ♦ *The name of the game is money, money, money.*

**nard guard** *n.* a male genital protector. ♦ *There was a nard guard attached to the center of the handlebars.*

**nature stop** *n.* a stop to use the toilet, especially during road travel. (Euphemistic.) ♦ *I think I need a nature stop when it's convenient.*

**naughty bits** *n.* genitals; breasts. (From a skit on *Monty Python's Flying Circus*, a popular late 1960–1970s BBC comedy series still seen worldwide in reruns.) ♦ *Those grape smugglers don't do much for the naughty bits.*

**neanderthal** [niˈændɚθɑl] *n.* a large and ugly male. (See also **cromagnon**.) ♦ *Tell that neanderthal to get out of here.*

nerd magnet

**Nebraska sign** *n.* a flat EEG indicating the death of the patient being monitored. (From the flatness of the state of Nebraska. Medical.) ♦ *I saw the Nebraska sign on my monitor and knew it must not be hooked up right.*

the **necessary** *n.* money; an income. (Also a really old term for a toilet or bathroom.) ♦ *I can always use more of the necessary.*

**negatory** *mod.* no; negative. ♦ Q: *Are you going to leave now?* A: *Negatory.*

**nerd magnet** *n.* a girl or woman who attracts dull males. ♦ *Sally is weary of dating total drips. She is a classic nerd magnet.*

**nerd mobile** *n.* a full-sized, uninteresting car; a family car. ♦ *My father always buys some kind of stupid nerd mobile.*

**nerd pack** *n.* a plastic sheath for holding pens in a pocket, protecting the cloth from ink. (This is the classic symbol of a bookish **nerd**.) ♦ *A real nerd wears a nerd pack in the pocket of a dirty shirt.*

**nicked** *mod.* arrested. ♦ *"Now I'm nicked," he said.*

**nippers** *n.* handcuffs; leg fetters. ♦ *No, not the nippers. They hurt my arms.*

**nipply** *mod.* [of weather] cold. (A play on *nippy [weather]* and what such weather may do to the human nipples.) ♦ *It's a little nipply out this morning.*

**nitery** ['naɪtɚi] *n.* a nightclub. ♦ *There is a cheap nitery over on Twelfth Street where Chuck has a job.*

**no big deal** AND **no biggie; no big whoop** *n.* (something) not difficult or troublesome. ♦ *Don't worry. It's no big deal.* ♦ *No biggie; no prob.*

**no go** ['no 'go] *mod.* negative; inopportune. (This is hyphenated before a nominal.) ♦ *We're in a no-go situation.*

**no great shakes** *phr.* someone or something not very good. (There is no affirmative version of this.) ♦ *Your idea is no great shakes, but we'll try it anyway.*

**no sale** *interj.* no. ♦ *I wanted to go to Florida for the holidays, but my father said, "No sale."*

**no sweat** *interj.* no problem; Don't worry; it is no problem. ♦ *It's no big deal. No sweat.*

**no-brainer** *n.* an easy question that takes no thinking to answer; a simple problem that requires no intellect to solve; a dilemma that requires no pondering to resolve.

♦ *His proposal of marriage was a no-brainer. She turned him down flat on the spot.*

**no-brow** *n.* a stupid person. (Patterned on **lowbrow**.) ♦ *Sam is a complete no-brow. No culture, no sense of style, and no money.*

**no-goodnik** [no'gʊdnɪk] *n.* someone who is no good. (The *nik* is from Russian via Yiddish.) ♦ *Tell the no-goodnik to leave quietly, or I will call the police.*

**noid** *n.* a *paranoid* person. ♦ *Some of those noids write hilarious letters to the editor.*

**noise 1.** *n.* empty talk; nonsense. ♦ *I've had enough of your noise. Shut up!* **2.** *n.* heroin. (Drugs.) ♦ *Man, I need some noise now! I hurt!*

**nosebleed seats** *n.* seats high up in an arena, theater, or opera house. ♦ *We could only afford the nosebleed seats for the opera.*

**nose-lunger** ['nozləŋɚ] *n.* a mass of nasal mucus. (See also **lunger**.) ♦ *Beavis thought the funniest thing in the world was having a nose-lunger dangling from his chin.*

**nosher** ['nɑʃɚ] *n.* someone who is always eating snacks. ♦ *I don't know of a single nosher who's not fat.*

**Not!** *interj.* Not really so! (A tag phrase added to the end of a statement, changing it from affirmative to negative. There is usually a pause before **Not!**, which is said on a level pitch somewhat higher than the sentence that comes before.) ♦ *Of course I'm going to pay $100 a ticket to see a rock concert. Not!*

**not know shit from shinola** *tv.* to know what's what; to be knowledgeable in the ways of the world. ♦ *That* *jerk doesn't know shit from shinola! Don't even ask him about it!*

**not too shabby 1.** *mod.* [with emphasis on *shabby*] nice; well done. ♦ *Is that your car? Not too shabby!* **2.** *mod.* [with emphasis on *too*] very shabby; very poor indeed. (Sarcastic.) ♦ *What a way to treat someone. Not too shabby!*

**notch** *tv.* to count up something; to add up or score something. ♦ *Well, it looks like we notched another victory.*

**nothing upstairs** *phr.* no brains; stupid. ♦ *Tom is sort of stupid acting. You know—nothing upstairs.* ♦ *I know what's wrong with you. Nothing upstairs.*

**nuggets** *n.* the testicles. ♦ *Man, my nuggets are cold! Let's hurry up and get back in the car.*

**nuke** *tv.* to microwave something. ♦ *I have to nuke my dinner and then I will be right over.*

**nuke** oneself [n(j)uk...] *tv.* to tan oneself at a tanning salon. ♦ *I nuke myself once a week in the spring so I will be ready for the summer bikini season.*

**nuker** ['n(j)ukɚ] *n.* a microwave oven. ♦ *I tried to do a turkey in the nuker once and made a real mess of it.*

**numbnuts** *n.* a jerk; a worthless person. (Usually a male.) ♦ *Hey, numbnuts! What did you do that for?*

**numero uno** ['numɚo 'uno] **1.** *n.* number one; the best. (Spanish.) ♦ *This coffee is numero uno in my book.* **2.** *n.* oneself; number one. ♦ *I always look out for numero uno.*

nuke

**nummy** ['nəmi] *tasty; yummy.* (Also juvenile or baby talk.) ♦ *Here, Jimmy, don't you want a spoon of this nummy food?*

**nunya** ['nən jə] *phr.* none of your [business]. ♦ *Nunya. Why do you want to know?*

**nutsack** *n.* the scrotum. ♦ *He's got an itch on the nutsack.*

**nutter** *n.* a nutty person. ♦ *That guy is a real nutter. Thinks he can get a cab at this hour.*

**nuttery** *n.* an insane asylum; the place where nuts are kept. ♦ *If you keep acting so odd, we'll have to put you in a nuttery.*

# O

**oak(s)** [oks] *mod.* OK; satisfactory; worthy. (Prisons.) ♦ *That dude's oaks.*

**oasis** [o'esəs] *n.* a place to buy liquor. ♦ *Let's go into this oasis here and pick up a few bottles.*

**ob** [ɑb] *mod.* obvious. ♦ *It's pretty ob that you are just trying to start something.*

**obno(c)** ['ɑbno AND 'ɑb'nɑk] *mod.* obnoxious; disgusting. ♦ *I wish you weren't so obnoc all the time!*

**obtanium** **1.** *n.* a substance or thing that can be obtained. ♦ *I need some kind of very strong glue. I don't know if it's obtanium.* **2.** *mod.* obtainable. ♦ *She's a beaut! Is she obtanium?*

**odd-bod** ['ɑdbɑd] **1.** *n.* a strange person. ♦ *Who is that odd-bod over in the corner?* **2.** *n.* a person with a strange body. ♦ *I am such an odd-bod that it's hard to find clothes that fit.* **3.** *n.* a peculiar body. ♦ *I have such an odd-bod that it's hard to find clothes.*

**off** one's **chump** *mod.* crazy; nuts. ♦ *Am I off my chump, or did that car suddenly disappear?*

**off** one's **meds** *phr.* acting strangely. ♦ *Man, what a temper! Must be off her meds.*

**off-brand cigarette** *n.* a marijuana cigarette. (Drugs.)
♦ *Shorty smokes nothing but those off-brand cigarettes.*

**oil it** *tv.* to study all night. (Literally, *burn the midnight oil.*) ♦ *I have a test tomorrow, and I really have to oil it tonight.*

**oink** [oɪŋk] *n.* a police officer. (A play on **pig**.) ♦ *There is an oink following us on a motorcycle!*

**oink out** *in.* to overeat. ♦ *This Thursday starts a four-day weekend, and I plan to oink out every day.*

**oinker** *n.* a very fat person. (Refers to the fatness of a pig.) ♦ *Who is that oinker who just came into the cafeteria? There won't be any food left for the rest of us.*

**OJ** *so tv.* to stab someone. (Refers to the O. J. Simpson stabbing case.) ♦ *Don't worry. I would never OJ my buddy.*

**old school** AND **old skool** *mod.* vintage; from an earlier time; retro. (Generally positive. As in the well-established expression from the old school.) ♦ *His way of dealing with people is strictly old school.*

**oldbie** *n.* someone who is not a **newbie**; someone who is not new to a group, place, activity, etc. ♦ *Speaking as an oldbie, I wish you newbies would RTFF!*

**on a tight leash** **1.** *mod.* under very careful control. ♦ *We can't do much around here. The boss has us all on a tight leash.* **2.** *mod.* addicted to some drug. ♦ *Wilmer is on a tight leash. He has to have the stuff regularly.*

**on fire** **1.** *mod.* very attractive or sexy. ♦ *Look at those jet-set people! Each one of them is just on fire.* **2.** *mod.* doing very well; very enthusiastic. ♦ *Fred is on fire in his new job. He'll get promoted in no time.*

**on ice** *mod.* in reserve. ♦ *That's a great idea, but we'll have to put it on ice until we can afford to put it into action.*

**on it** *mod.* really good. ♦ *Man, Weasel is really on it! What a rad lad!*

**on** one's **own hook** *mod.* all by oneself. ♦ *I don't need any help. I can do it on my own hook.*

**on** so's **watch** *mod.* while someone is on duty. ♦ *I guess I have to bear the blame since it happened on my watch.*

**on tap 1.** *mod.* having to do with beer sold from a barrel or keg. ♦ *Do you have any imported beers on tap here?* **2.** *mod.* immediately available. ♦ *I have just the kind of person you're talking about on tap.*

**on task** *mod.* paying attention to the job at hand. ♦ *I find it hard to stay on task with all those babes going by.*

**on the bird** *mod.* available on the TV satellite channels. ♦ *There is a whole lot of good stuff on the bird, but you need a receiving dish to get it.*

**on the DL** *mod.* as a secret; secretly; on the QT. (From *down low.*) ♦ *She'll get in trouble because they did it on the DL.*

**on the gooch** *mod.* true. ♦ *What I'm telling you is on the gooch, for sure.*

**on the make** *mod.* ambitious; attempting to be great. ♦ *That young lawyer is sure on the make.*

**on the mojo** […'modʒo] *mod.* addicted to morphine; using morphine. (Drugs. See also **mojo**.) ♦ *How long you been on the mojo?*

**on the outs (with so)** *mod.* in a mild dispute with someone; sharing ill will with someone. ♦ *Tom has been on the outs with Bill before. They'll work it out.*

**on the rezzie** *mod.* right; true. ♦ *What I'm telling you is on the rezzie, for sure.*

**on the rilla** *mod.* truly; true. (Possibly related to *really*.) ♦ *On the rilla, he really did it!*

**on the same page** *mod.* have the same understanding or amount of knowledge. (As if people were reading from the same page.) ♦ *We're not on the same page. Listen carefully to what I am telling you.*

**on the same wavelength** *mod.* thinking in the same pattern. ♦ *We're not on the same wavelength. Let's try again.*

**on the squiff** […skwɪf] *mod.* on a drinking bout. ♦ *Shorty is always on the squiff, except when he's shooting dope.*

**on the wires** *mod.* using the telephone. (Landline or cellphone.) ♦ *She can't talk to you now. She's on the wires.*

**On your bike!** AND **Go to your room!** *imperative* Get out of here!; Go away and stop bothing me. (Neither is to be taken literally.) ♦ *What a bad joke! No puns allowed here! On your bike!* ♦ *Nasty mouth! Such talk! Go to your room!*

**on your six** *phr.* [look] behind you. (At one's *six o'clock*.) ♦ *Look out! On your six!*

**one smart apple** *n.* a smart or clever person. ♦ *That Sue is one smart apple.*

**one-finger salute** AND **OFS** *phr. & comp. abb.* the finger; the *digitus impudicus.* ♦ *And an OFS to you, sir.*

**onto** so/sth *mod.* alerted to or aware of a deceitful plan or person. ♦ *Wilmer thought he was safe, but the fuzz was onto him from the beginning.*

**oof** [uf] **1.** *exclam.* the sound one makes when one is struck in the abdomen. (Usually **Oof!**) ♦ *"Oof!" cried Tom. He couldn't talk any more after that.* **2.** *n.* the potency of the alcohol in liquor; the effect of potent alcohol. ♦ *This stuff really has oof. How old is it?*

**OOSOOM** Go to out of sight, out of mind.

**OP's** ['o'piz] *n.* other people's cigarettes; begged or borrowed cigarettes. (Initialism.) ♦ *My favorite kind of cigarettes is OP's. They're the cheapest, too.*

**org** [org] **1.** *n.* the **rush** caused by potent drugs. (Drugs. From *orgasm.*) ♦ *Bart hated the vomiting when he first took it, but he loved the org.* **2.** *n.* an organization. (Also the internet domain ".org" often assigned to nonprofit organizations.) ♦ *She's a member of the org and can't be expected to use independent judgment.*

**organic** *mod.* great. ♦ *This is one fine, organic rally! I'm glad I stopped by.*

**ossified** ['ɑsəfaɪd] *mod.* alcohol or drug intoxicated. (From **stoned (out)**.) ♦ *How can anybody be so ossified on four beers?*

**Otis** ['otɪs] **1.** *n.* a drunkard. (From the name of a television character who is the town drunk. Also a term of address.) ♦ *Look at Otis over there, propped up against the wall.* **2.** *mod.* drunk. ♦ *Fred was Otis by midnight and began looking like he was going to barf.*

**OTL** ['o'ti'ɛl] *phr.* out to lunch; spacy; giddy. (An initialism.) ♦ *Sue is OTL. She seems witless all the time.*

**OTOH** *phr.* on the other hand. (An initialism. A computer abbreviation, not pronounced.) ♦ *That's one good idea. OTOH, there must be many other satisfactory procedures.*

**out of left field** *mod.* suddenly; from an unexpected source or direction. ♦ *All of his paintings are right out of left field.*

**out of sight, out of mind** AND **OOSOOM** *phr. & comp. abb.* I don't pay attention to what I can't see. ♦ *I completely forgot about it. OOSOOM!*

**out of sync** [...sɪŋk] *mod.* uncoordinated; unsynchronized. ♦ *My watch and your watch are out of sync.*

**out the gazoo** [...gə'zu] *phr.* in great plenty; everywhere. (Gazoo = anus. Usually objectionable.) ♦ *We have old magazines out the gazoo here. Can't we throw some of them away?*

**out to lunch** *mod.* absentminded; giddy; stupid acting. (See also OTL.) ♦ *Old Ted is so out to lunch these days. Seems to be losing his mind.*

**out-and-out** *mod.* complete or total; blatant. ♦ *Don't be such an out-and-out stinker!*

**outed 1.** AND **offed** *mod.* dead; killed. ♦ *The witness was offed before a subpoena could be issued.* **2.** *mod.* having had one's homosexual identity made public. (Not prenominal.) ♦ *Yes, he's outed, but he hasn't told his parents.*

**outfit 1.** *n.* a group of people; a company. ♦ *That outfit cheated me out of my money.* **2.** *n.* a set of clothing. ♦ *You look lovely in that outfit.* **3.** *n.* a set of things; the items needed for some task. ♦ *My tool kit has everything I need. It's the whole outfit.*

**overkill** *n.* too much. ♦ *That is enough. Any more is just overkill.*

**overserved** *mod.* having to do with a drunken person in a bar; alcohol intoxicated. (Euphemistic.) ♦ *The overserved guy there in the corner is going to be sick.*

**owl-prowl** *n.* a nighttime session of owl watching. (Bird watchers humor.) ♦ *We went on an owl-prowl last night and spotted a spotted owl. It was a barn owl, but we spotted it.*

**ownage** *n.* an instance of owning something; an instance of dominating something; the acquisition of control over something. ♦ *This whole idea was mine and I am still in control. This is an extreme case of ownage.*

# P

**pad down (somewhere)** *in.* to make one's bed somewhere, usually a casual or temporary bed. ♦ *Do you mind if I pad down at your place for the night?*

**pad out** *in.* to go to bed or to sleep. ♦ *Man, if I don't pad out by midnight, I'm a zombie.*

**padded** *mod.* plump or fat. ♦ *He didn't hurt himself when he fell down. He's well padded there.*

**paid** *mod.* alcohol intoxicated. ♦ *I think I'll go out and get paid tonight.*

**paint 1.** *n.* a tattoo. ♦ *When dya get the new paint?* **2.** *n.* tattoos in general; the amount of tattooing on someone's body. ♦ *He's got paint covering his back!*

**palm** *tv.* to conceal something in the hand as in a theft or the performance of a magic trick; to receive and conceal a tip or a bribe. ♦ *The kid palmed the candy bar and walked right out of the store.*

**palsy-walsy** ['pælzi'wælzi] **1.** *n.* a good friend, **pal**, or buddy. (Also a term of address.) ♦ *Meet my old palsy-walsy, John. We've known each other since we were kids.* **2.** *mod.* friendly; overly friendly. (Often with *with*.) ♦ *Why is Tom so palsy-walsy with everyone?*

**panic** *n.* a very funny or exciting person or thing. ♦ *Paul is a panic. He tells a joke a minute.*

**pants rabbits** *n.* lice. (See also seam-squirrels. Contrived.) ♦ *Bart is sure scratching a lot. Do you think he's got pants rabbits?*

**paperweight** *n.* a serious student; a hardworking student. ♦ *What a jerk! Nothing but a paperweight.*

**park the pink Plymouth** *n.* to copulate. ♦ *He set out to park the pink Plymouth but ended up in a train wreck.*

**partay** ['pɑr 'tei] *in.* to party; to celebrate. ♦ *Time to partay!*

**party animal** *n.* someone who loves parties. ♦ *My boyfriend and I are real party animals. Let's party!*

**Party on!** *exclam.* That's right! ♦ *Party on, Beavis! You are totally right!*

**pass go** *tv.* to complete a difficult or dangerous task successfully. (From *pass go and collect $200* in the game Monopoly.) ♦ *You had better pass go with this job, or you've had it.*

**passy** *n.* a baby's pacifier. (Baby talk.) ♦ *Does little Johnnie want his passy?*

**paste** sth **on** so **1.** *tv.* to charge someone with a crime. ♦ *You can't paste that charge on me! Max did it!* **2.** *tv.* to land a blow on someone. ♦ *If you do that again, I'll paste one on you.*

**pay the water bill** *tv.* to urinate. ♦ *I'll be with you as soon as I pay the water bill.*

**p-crutch** *n.* a police car. (Streets. **Crutch** = car.) ♦ *Hey, bro, there's a p-crutch behind you.*

**peace out** *in.* to depart; to leave. ♦ *Let's peace out. It's too hot in here.*

**peanut head** *n.* an oaf; a nerd. ♦ *You are so silly, Kim. You're a real peanut head!*

**pecker slap 1.** *n.* an act of striking a male in the genitals. **2.** *tv.* to strike a male in the genitals. ♦ *We'll pecker slap those guys with every dodge ball we throw.*

**peckish** *mod.* hungry. ♦ *I'm just a little peckish right now. I need a bite to eat.*

**pecks** AND **pecs; pects** [pɛk(t)s] *n.* the pectoral muscles. (From weightlifting and bodybuilding.) ♦ *Look at the pecks on that guy!*

**peg out** *in.* to die. ♦ *I was so scared, I thought I would peg out for sure.*

**peg so** *tv.* to gossip about someone. ♦ *Kim is always pegging Jill. What's her problem?*

**penis wrinkle** *n.* a despised person, usually a male. (Also a term of address.) ♦ *Get out of here, penis wrinkle.*

**penny** *n.* a police officer. (A play on **copper**.) ♦ *The penny over on the corner told the boys to get moving.*

**people processor** *n.* a nickname for an airplane propeller. (Used by people who have an occasion to get near one while it is spinning.) ♦ *Watch out for the people processor at the front end.*

**perma-fried** *mod.* very drunk or drug intoxicated; very fried. ♦ *She got herself perma-fried and couldn't drive home.*

**phat blunt** *n.* a fat marijuana cigarette. (*Phat is fat.*) ♦ *Man, that's a phat blunt!*

**phat-phree** *mod.* not cool; not PHAT. (A play on *fat-free.*) ♦ *We had to read some stupid, phat-phree play by some old homie called Jakespeer.*

**phazed** AND **phased** [fezd] *mod.* intoxicated with marijuana. ♦ *How much booze does it take you to get really phased?*

**phish** AND **spoof; card** *in.* to "fish" for passwords and personal information by trickery, on internet. (Sometimes by setting up a phony URL which people sign in to by giving their passwords or credit card numbers.) ♦ *They must have been phishing to get my credit card number while I placed an order online.*

**phreak** *n.* a respelling of *freak.* ♦ *You stupid freak! Why'd you do that?*

**phumfed** ['fəm(p)ft] *mod.* drug intoxicated. ♦ *You can't get your work done when you are totally phumfed.*

**phutz** AND **futz** [fəts] *tv.* to rob, swindle, or cheat someone. ♦ *Don't futz me! Tell the truth!*

**piccie** *n.* a little picture; a thumbnail picture. ♦ *Put some piccies on your web page. That'll brighten it up.*

**pig heaven** *n.* a police station. (Chiefly black.) ♦ *All the bacon eventually goes home to pig heaven.*

**pig out** *in.* to overeat; to overindulge in food or drink. (See also **blimp out**; **scarf out**.) ♦ *I can't help myself when I see ice cream. I have to pig out.*

**pigeon-eyed** *mod.* alcohol intoxicated. ♦ *Who is that pigeon-eyed guy over there who is having such a hard time standing up?*

**pigmobile** *n.* a police car. ♦ *Look out, here comes the pig-mobile!*

**pigpen** *n.* a crosshatch or the number sign: #. (Computers.) ♦ *There is nothing on my printout but a whole string of pigpens.*

**pilfered** ['pɪlfɚd] *mod.* alcohol intoxicated. ♦ *I've had too much. I'm beginning to feel pilfered.*

**pillage** *tv.* to eat a meal, perhaps by raiding a refrigerator. (Perhaps voraciously.) ♦ *Let's go pillage Tom's fridge. I'm hungarian.*

**pillowed** *mod.* pregnant. (Refers to the swelling in a pregnant woman's abdomen.) ♦ *She does look a bit pillowed, doesn't she?*

**pimp steak** *n.* a hot dog; a wiener. ♦ *Oh, no! Not pimp steak again tonight.*

**pimpish** ['pɪmpɪʃ] *mod.* flamboyant in dress and manner, as with a pimp. (Use caution with **pimp** and the topic.) ♦ *Take the feathers off it, and it won't look quite so pimpish.*

**pimpmobile** *n.* a gaudy automobile, as might be driven by a **pimp**. (Use caution with **pimp**.) ♦ *He drove up in a pimpmobile and shocked all the neighbors.*

**ping** SO *tv.* to get someone's attention, via computer or otherwise. ♦ *I saw her on the other side of the room and pinged her.*

**pinked** *mod.* alcohol intoxicated; tipsy. ♦ *She's sitting there looking a bit pinked.*

**pinstriper** *n.* a businessman or businesswoman wearing a pinstriped suit. (From men's pinstripe business suits.) ♦ *Who's the pinstriper driving the beemer?*

**piss around** *in.* to waste time; to be inefficient at something. (Usually objectionable.) ♦ *She's just pissing around. She'll never finish.*

**piss blood 1.** *tv.* to experience great anxiety. (Usually objectionable.) ♦ *He made me piss blood before he agreed.* **2.** *tv.* to expend an enormous amount of energy. (Usually objectionable.) ♦ *I pissed blood to come in first in the race.*

**piss elegant** *mod.* very pretentious; overly elegant. (Usually objectionable.) ♦ *Man, this place is piss elegant. Look at them lamp shades!*

**piss factory** *n.* a bar, tavern, or saloon. (Usually objectionable.) ♦ *I stopped in at the piss factory for a round or two.*

**piss off** AND **PO** *in.* to depart; to go away. (Objectionable to many people.) ♦ *Piss off, you jerk! Get out!*

**piss quiz** *n.* a urine test for drugs. (Usually objectionable.) ♦ *They told me I had to take a piss quiz to work there.*

**piss** so **off** *tv.* to make someone angry. (Potentially offensive, even though it is widely used. See also **pissed (off)**.) ♦ *She really pissed me off!*

**piss** sth **away** *tv.* to waste all of something, such as time or money. (Usually objectionable.) ♦ *He pissed away the best possible chances.*

**piss-cutter** AND **piss-whiz** *n.* an extraordinary person; someone who can do the impossible. (Usually objectionable.) ♦ *Sam is a real piss-cutter when it comes to running.* ♦ *I ain't no piss-whiz, just your average guy.*

**pissed 1.** *mod.* alcohol intoxicated. (Usually objectionable.) ♦ *He was so pissed he could hardly stand up.* **2.** *mod.* angry. (Potentially offensive, even though it is heard widely. See also **piss** so **off**.) ♦ *I was so pissed I could have screamed.*

**pissed (off) (at** so/sth**)** AND **pissed off about** so/sth *mod.* very angry with or about someone or something. (Objectionable to many people, but heard in all popular entertainment, schools, and the workplace.) ♦ *She's always so pissed off about something.* ♦ *He always seems pissed off at somebody.*

**pissing** *mod.* worthless; minimal. (Usually objectionable.) ♦ *I got a pissing amount of coffee for a buck and a quarter.*

**pissing-match** *n.* an argument; a pointless competition. (Usually objectionable.) ♦ *Let's call a halt to this pissing-match and get to work.*

**pissovers** *n.* briefs with no fly. (Usually objectionable.) ♦ *Charlie always wears pissovers. He hates boxers.*

**pistol** *n.* a person who is bright, quick, or energetic. (Implying *hot as a pistol* or *quick as a pistol*.) ♦ *Ask that pistol to step over here for a minute, would you?*

**pitch character** *n.* a person, animal, or cartoon character who delivers the major selling message in an advertisement. ♦ *You can't use a frog for a pitch character in a beer commercial!*

**pix** [pɪks] *n.* pictures; photographs. ♦ *Hold still and let me get your pix taken. Then you can jump around.*

**pizzazz** [pəˈzæz] *n.* punch; glitter and excitement. ♦ *Listen to the way she put pizzazz into that song!*

**plastic 1.** *mod.* phony; false. ♦ *She wears too much makeup and looks totally plastic.* **2.** *n.* a plastic credit card. ♦ *I don't carry any cash, just plastic.* **3.** *mod.* having to do with credit cards and their use. ♦ *There is too much plastic debt in most households.*

**plastic punk** *n.* falsely stylish. ♦ *Isn't all punk really plastic punk?*

**play ball (with** so**)** *tv.* to cooperate with someone. ♦ *Are you going to play ball, or do I have to report you to the boss?*

**play hide the sausage** *tv.* to perform an act of copulation. (Jocular. Usually objectionable.) ♦ *Then he said he wanted to play hide the sausage.*

**play hooky** [...ˈhʊki] *tv.* to not go to school; to not keep an appointment. ♦ *I played hooky today and did not go to work.*

**play in the big leagues** *in.* to become involved in something of large or important proportions. ♦ *The conduc-*

*tor shouted at the oboist, "You're playing in the big leagues now. Tune up or ship out."*

**play tonsil hockey** *tv.* to kiss deeply, using the tongue. ♦ *Kids sit around in cars, playing tonsil hockey all evening.*

**play with a full deck** *in.* to operate as if one were mentally sound. (Usually in the negative. One cannot play cards with a partial deck.) ♦ *Look sharp, you dummies! Pretend you are playing with a full deck.*

**playa 1.** *n.* an active and popular man or woman. ♦ *She's dressed to be a playa.* **2.** *n.* someone who is skilled and respected as a successful street con; pimp; dealer; womanizer, etc. ♦ *Sam is a real playa and already has eight kids.*

**playa hata** *n.* someone who does not respect or is jealous of a playa. ♦ *The dude is just a playa hata. Has something against success.*

**plonko** *n.* a drunkard. ♦ *Get that smelly plonko out of here!*

**plootered** ['pludɚd] *mod.* alcohol intoxicated. ♦ *We went out and got totally plootered.*

**plowing water** *n.* wasting time doing something futile. ♦ *You're wasting your time. You're plowing water.*

**plumber's smile** AND **working man's smile** *n.* the upper part of the gluteal cleft visible above the beltline of a man, bent over at work. *I came into the kitchen and was greeted by a plumber's smile owned by some guy working under the sink.* ♦ *She referred to the overexposure of his rear end over his belt as the "working man's smile."*

**pocket of time** *n.* a period of available time, as might be found between appointments. ♦ *I had a pocket of time between stops that I used to get myself one of those incredibly expensive cups of coffee.*

**pocket pool** *n.* the act of a male playing with his genitals with his hand in his pants pocket. (Usually objectionable.) ♦ *Stop playing pocket pool and get to work.*

**pocket-rocket** *n.* the penis. (Usually objectionable.) ♦ *He held his hands over his pocket-rocket and ran for the bedroom.*

**poindexter** ['pɔindɛkstɚ] *n.* a bookish person; a well-mannered good student, usually male. (Also a term of address.) ♦ *I'm no poindexter. In fact, my grades are pretty low.*

**point man 1.** *n.* a ballplayer who habitually scores points. ♦ *Fred is supposed to be point man for our team, but tonight he is not doing so well.* **2.** *n.* anyone whose job it is to score successes against the opposition. ♦ *The president expects the secretary of defense to be point man for this new legislation.*

**pole dancer** *n.* a woman, thought of as a stripper, who performs erotic dances around a metal pole, onstage, exploiting the pole's phallic form. ♦ *Jed swears that he has never seen an inept pole dancer.*

**polluted** *mod.* alcohol or drug intoxicated. ♦ *Those guys are really polluted.*

**pond scum** *n.* a mean and wretched person; a worthless male. (Collegiate. An elaboration of **scum**, less crude than **scumbag**. Also a rude term of address.) ♦ *Get your hands off me, you pond scum!*

**poop chute** *n.* the rectum and anus. ♦ *The doctor actually stuck his finger up my poop chute.*

**pooper** *n.* the buttocks. ♦ *How is she going to get that humongous pooper into the chair?*

**poot** *in.* to break wind; to fart. ♦ *Who pooted?*

**pop for** sth *in.* to pay for a treat (for someone). ♦ *Let's have some ice cream. I'll pop for it.*

**popcorn pimp** *n.* a pimp who runs a small operation. (Streets. *Popcorn* here means small; as in *popcorn shrimp*.) ♦ *Reggie is nothing but a popcorn pimp. He'll never amount to much.*

**popo** *n.* (Streets.) the police. ♦ *The popo just picked up that stewed dude.*

**popping** *in.* happening. ♦ *Things are always popping at the gym.*

**pops** *n.* one's father; any older man. (Also a term of address.) ♦ *Hey, pops! How you doing?*

**pork hammer** *n.* the penis. ♦ *Stop scratching your pork hammer, bro.*

**porker** *n.* a fat person. ♦ *Sally is not exactly a porker, but she is not skinny either.*

**pository** *mod.* yes; positive. ♦ Q: *Is this the right one?* A: *Pository.*

**potato soup** *n.* vodka. (This liquor is typically made from potatoes.) ♦ *Have a bit of this potato soup, why don't you?*

**POTS** *n.* plain old telephone service [for a computer connection to the Internet]. (As opposed to connection through a TV cable or high-speed telephone line.) ♦ *Even in five years, most people will still rely on POTS to get connected to the Internet.*

**pound** one's **ear** *tv.* to sleep. ♦ *She went home to pound her ear an hour or two before work.*

**pounds** *n.* dollars; money. ♦ *How many pounds does this thing cost?*

**powder up** *in.* to drink heavily; to get drunk. ♦ *He's at the tavern powdering up.*

**power tool** *n.* a student who studies most of the time. (An elaboration of **tool**.) ♦ *Willard is a power tool if there ever was one. Studies most of the night.*

**powerstudy** *n.* to study hard. ♦ *I've got to powerstudy for the exam. I haven't cracked a book all semester.*

**poz** *mod.* HIV positive. ♦ *He was afraid he would turn up poz.*

**prairie dog** *in.* [for people in office cubicles] to pop up to see what's going on in the rest of the office. ♦ *Everybody was prairie dogging to see what was going on.*

**prayerbones** *n.* the knees. ♦ *He pushed one of his prayerbones into my gut.*

**presenteeism** *n.* the affliction of failing to take time off from work, even when it is available. (A jocular and contrived opposite of *absenteeism*.) ♦ *The office suffered from bouts of presenteeism during the winter when the workload was light.*

**President Wilson** *n.* an erection. (Punning on *Woodrow* = **woody** Wilson.) ♦ *I am always happy to see President Wilson come round.*

prairie dogging

**primo** ['primo] *mod.* great; first-class. ♦ *This pizza is really primo.*

**props** *n.* evidence of respect; one's proper respect. ♦ *You gotta give me my props.*

**pseudo** ['sudo] **1.** *mod.* false; bogus. ♦ *This is a very pseudo position that you are taking.* **2.** *n.* a phony person. ♦ *Randy is such a pseudo! What a fake!*

**pudding ring** *n.* a mustache and goatee, grown together to form a circle. He worked and worked to get his "pudding ring" just right, then got a huge zit that ruined the whole thing.

**puff** *in.* to get drunk. ♦ *Those guys go out and puff every Friday night.*

**Puh-leez!** [pəə 'liiiz] *exclam.* Please!; That is enough! You can't expect me to accept that! (A long, drawn-out way of saying *Please!* The tone of voice shows exasperation and disgust. The spelling is highly variable.) ♦ *I am the one who's at fault? Puuuleeeze!*

**pukish** *mod.* nauseated. (Folksy.) ♦ *That old pukish feeling came over me, and I just let go.*

**pull chocks** AND **pull up stakes** *tv.* to leave a place. (*Chocks* refer to blocks that keep wheels from rolling, and *stakes* refers to tent stakes.) ♦ *Time to pull chocks and get out of here.* ♦ *We pulled up stakes and moved on.*

**pump 1.** *tv.* to press someone for an answer or information. ♦ *Don't pump me! I will tell you nothing!* **2.** *n.* the heart. ♦ *He has the pump of a forty-year-old.* **3.** *n.* a pumped-up muscle. (Bodybuilding.) ♦ *He's tired and can't quite make a pump.*

**pump ship 1.** *tv.* to urinate. (Crude. From an expression meaning to pump the bilge water from a ship.) ♦ *He stopped and pumped ship right in the alley.* **2.** *tv.* to empty one's stomach; to vomit. (Crude. Less well known than the previous sense.) ♦ *After I pumped ship, I felt better.*

**pump (some) iron** *tv.* to lift weights. ♦ *Andy went down to the gym to pump some iron.*

**punch** SO's **lights out** *tv.* to knock someone out; to close someone's eyes with a hard blow. ♦ *Shut up, or I'll punch your lights out.*

**punk out 1.** *in.* to chicken out. ♦ *He was supposed to ask her out, but he punked out at the last minute.* **2.** *in.* to become a **punker**. ♦ *If my kids ever punked out and looked like that, I think I'd clobber them.*

**purple kush** *n.* marijuana. ♦ *He's high on purple kush.*

**push money** *n.* extra money paid to a salesperson to sell certain merchandise aggressively. (See also **spiff**.) ♦ *The manufacturer supplied a little push money that even the store manager didn't know about.*

**pussy-whipped** *mod.* [of a male] dominated or controlled by a woman. ♦ *Your trouble is that you're pussy-whipped, Casper.*

**put a con on** so *tv.* to attempt to deceive someone; to attempt to swindle someone. (Underworld.) ♦ *Don't try to put a con on me, Buster! I've been around too long.*

**put balls on** sth *tv.* to make something more masculine or powerful; to give something authority and strength. (Usually objectionable.) ♦ *Come on, sing louder. Put some balls on it.*

**put the arm on** so **1.** *tv.* to demand something of someone, especially money. ♦ *I know Tom wants some money. He put the arm on me, but I said no.* **2.** *tv.* to arrest someone. (Underworld.) ♦ *They put the arm on Bart for pushing pills.*

**put the chill on** so AND **put the freeze on** so *tv.* to ignore someone. ♦ *She was pretty snooty till we all put the chill on her.* ♦ *Why are you guys putting the freeze on me? What I do?*

**put the clamps on** so/sth AND **put the clamps on** *tv.* to impede or block someone or something; to restrain or restrict someone. ♦ *Fred had to put the clamps on Tony, who was rushing his work too much.*

**put the kibosh on** sth *tv.* to squelch something. ♦ *The mayor put the kibosh on the whole deal.*

**put the moves on** so *tv.* to attempt to seduce someone. (With *any* in the negative.) ♦ *If somebody doesn't try to put the moves on her, she thinks she's a failure.*

**put to it** *mod.* in trouble or difficulty; hard up (for something such as money). (As if one's back were put to the wall.) ♦ *Sorry, I can't lend you anything. I'm a bit put to it this month.*

**put your hands together for** so AND **put them together for** so *tv.* to applaud someone. (To put hands together clapping.) ♦ *Please put your hands together for Ronald and his great musicians!*

**putrid** *mod.* alcohol intoxicated. ♦ *That guy is stinking drunk. Putrid, in fact.*

**putt-putt** *n.* a small motorized vehicle, especially a small car. ♦ *That's not a motorcycle; it's just a little putt-putt.*

**putz around** AND **futz around** *in.* to waste time; to do something ineffectually. ♦ *Get busy and stop putzing around.*

**pythons** *n.* large, muscular biceps. (See also **guns**.) ♦ *Look at the pythons on that guy! He could lift a piano!*

# Q

**quads** *n.* the quadriceps, large muscles in the upper legs. (Bodybuilding.) ♦ *I found some great new exercises to strengthen my quads.*

**qual** [kwɑl] *n.* qualitative analysis. (Scientific.) ♦ *We'll have to turn to qual for that answer.*

**quant 1.** AND **quan** *n.* quantitative analysis. (Scientific and collegiate.) ♦ *I didn't study enough for my quant test.* **2.** *n.* a technician who works in securities market analysis. ♦ *He was a quant on Wall Street for two years.*

**quarterback** *tv.* to manage, lead, or direct someone or something. ♦ *I quarterbacked the whole company for more years than I care to remember.*

**Que pasa?** [ke ˈpɑsə] *interrog.* Hello, what's going on? (Spanish.) ♦ *Hey, man! Que pasa?*

**queer for** sth *mod.* in the mood for something; desiring something. ♦ *She's queer for him because of his money.*

**queer-beer 1.** *n.* bad beer; beer of low alcohol content. ♦ *I hate this queer-beer. Get out the good stuff.* **2.** *n.* any strange person. (Also a term of address.) ♦ *What does that queer-beer think he's doing?* **3.** *mod.* having to do with homosexuals; homosexual. (Usually derogatory. Resented by homosexuals.) ♦ *I won't wear that queer-*

*beer outfit!* **4.** *n.* a homosexual male, possibly a female. (See sense 3.) ♦ *They say she's a queer-beer.*

**quick one** AND **quickie 1.** *n.* a quick drink of booze; a single beer consumed rapidly. ♦ *I could use a quickie about now.* **2.** *n.* a quick sex act. (Usually objectionable.) ♦ *They're in the bedroom having a quick one.*

**quick-and-dirty** *mod.* rapidly and carelessly done. ♦ *I'm selling this car, so all I want is a quick-and-dirty repair job.*

**quimp** [kmɪmp] *n.* a total jerk; a social outcast. (Also a term of address.) ♦ *I don't want to live in a dorm full of quimps.*

**quote, unquote** *phr.* a parenthetical expression said before a word or short phrase indicating that the word or phrase would be in quotation marks if used in writing. ♦ *So I said to her, quote, unquote, it's time we had a little talk.*

# R

**rack 1.** *n.* a bed. ♦ *You don't get to see the rack very much in the army.* **2.** *n.* a pair of [female] breasts. (Usually objectionable.) ♦ *Look at the rack on that dame! How can she stand upright?*

**rack face** *n.* one's face after sleeping in a bed or **rack**. ♦ *In the mirror, I saw an old man with "rack face" and a scraggly beard.*

**rack time** AND **rack duty** *n.* time spent in bed. (Military.) ♦ *Gee, I need some more rack time.* ♦ *I was on rack duty for my entire leave.*

**rackage** *n.* the female bosom; a set of breasts; a **rack**. ♦ *He stood there admiring all the boss rackage on the beach.*

**racked** *mod.* struck in the testicles. (Usually objectionable.) ♦ *The quarterback got racked and didn't play the rest of the quarter.*

**rad** [ræd] **1.** *n.* a radical person. (California.) ♦ *My brother is a rad, but he's a good guy.* **2.** *mod.* great; wonderful; excellent; exciting. (California. From **radical**.) ♦ *Oh my God, that's, like, really rad!*

**radical** *mod.* great; excellent. (California.) ♦ *My boyfriend, he's, like, so radical!*

**rage** *in.* to party; to celebrate. (Collegiate.) ♦ *Fred and Mary were raging over at the frat house last weekend.*

**rainbow** *n.* a bowlegged person. (Also a rude term of address.) ♦ *Ask that rainbow if he has to have special trousers made.*

**raisin ranch** *n.* a retirement community; an old folks home. (Refers to wrinkles.) ♦ *You won't get me into one of those raisin ranches. I like my independence.*

**rally** ['ræli] **1.** *n.* get-together of some kind; a party, usually informal, possibly spontaneous. ♦ *There's a rally over at Tom's tonight.* **2.** *in.* to hold a get-together of some kind; to **party**. (Collegiate.) ♦ *Let's rally tonight about midnight.*

**ralph** AND **rolf** [rælf AND rɔlf] *in.* to empty one's stomach; to vomit. (Teens and collegiate.) ♦ *She went home and ralphed for an hour.*

**rambo(ize)** ['ræmbo(ɑɪz)] *tv.* to (figuratively) annihilate someone or something; to harm someone or something. (Collegiate. From the powerful film character Rambo.) ♦ *The students ramboed the cafeteria, and the cops were called.*

**rammy** ['ræmi] *mod.* sexually excited or aroused. (Refers to the ram, a symbol of arousal.) ♦ *Fred was looking a little rammy, so I excused myself and left.*

**ranch 1.** *n.* semen. (Alludes to Ranch [salad] dressing. Objectionable if understood.) ♦ *God! There's ranch on the bathroom floor!* **2.** *in.* to ejaculate. (Objectionable if understood.) ♦ *Just looking at her makes me want to ranch.*

**rank** *tv.* to give someone a hard time; to **hassle** someone. (Possible from *pull rank* = use rank to dominate someone.) ♦ *Stop ranking me!*

**rasty** ['ræsti] *mod.* having to do with a harsh-looking young woman. (Collegiate.) ♦ *Who is that rasty dame I saw you with?*

**ratted** *mod.* drunk. ♦ *I think you are too ratted to drive.*

**rave** *n.* a party; a wild celebration. ♦ *Let's have a little rave next Friday.*

**Read the fucking FAQ!** AND **RTFF; RTFFAQ** *exclam. & comp. abb.* Simply read the information in the FAQ, Frequently Asked Questions. (Usually objectionable.) ♦ *Don't ask the group to explain everything just for you! RTFF!*

**Read the fucking manual!** AND **RTFM** *exclam. & comp. abb.* Simply read the manual and stop asking someone else to explain it to you! (Usually objectionable.) ♦ *Why should I write you a how-to book? RTFM!*

**real** *mod.* very; really. ♦ *This is a real fine party.*

**red gravy** *n.* blood. ♦ *If you're gonna pick your scabs, keep your red gravy and stuff off me!*

**redonkulous** *mod.* ridiculous. (Many variations.) ♦ *What a redonkulous thing to say!*

**refi** *n.* refinancing. ♦ *I've done three refis in the past two years. I still owe as much as I started with, but my payments are lower.*

**regs** *n.* regulations. ♦ *There is a list of regs posted on the back of your door.*

**rep** [rɛp] **1.** *n.* a representative, usually a sales representative. ♦ *Please ask your rep to stop by my office.* **2.** *n.* someone's reputation. ♦ *I've got my own rep to think about.* **3.** *n.* repertory theater. ♦ *Rep is the best place to get experience, but not to make connections.* **4.** *n.* Go to reps.

**rep out** *in.* to do too many repetitions of an exercise and reach exhaustion. ♦ *After forty crunches, he repped out. He's got some work to do.*

**reps** *n.* repetitions of an exercise. (Bodybuilding.) ♦ *After twenty reps, I think I could just keep going.*

**ret** [rɛt] *n.* a tobacco cigarette. (Collegiate.) ♦ *Give my buddy a ret, will you?*

**rhoid** *n.* a bothersome person; a person who is a pain in the ass. (From *hemorrhoid*.) ♦ *Get away from me, you rhoid!*

**rice-rocket** *n.* a Japanese motorcycle; a **crotch-rocket** from Japan. ♦ *He added a crack-rack to his rice-rocket.*

**ricockulous** *mod.* ridiculous. (Word play based on **dick** = cock.) ♦ *What a stupid thing to say! That is ricockulous!*

**ridic** *mod.* ridiculous. ♦ *What nonsense! That's so ridic!*

**riffed 1.** *mod.* alcohol or drug intoxicated. ♦ *I can't keep getting riffed every night like this.* **2.** AND **rift** *mod.* fired; released from employment. (From RIF, "reduction in force." A dismissal not for cause, but simply to reduce the number of workers.) ♦ *Most of the sales force was rift last week.*

**right guy** *n.* a good guy; a straight guy. ♦ *Tom is a right guy. No trouble with him.*

**rinky-dink** ['rɪŋki'dɪŋk] *mod.* cheap; inferior; broken down. ♦ *I sold my rinky-dink old car yesterday.*

**ritzy** ['rɪtsi] *mod.* elegant; flamboyant. ♦ *That is a real ritzy car.*

**rivets** ['rɪvəts] *n.* dollars; money. (From copper rivets.) ♦ *You got enough rivets on you for a snack?*

**rizzi** *n.* a means of transportation; a car. (Streets. Probably from *rizzle* = ride.) ♦ *Sammy's got himself a new rizzi.*

**roach-coach** *n.* a mobile snack truck. (The term was revived in the Persian Gulf War.) ♦ *The roach-coach pulled up in front of the dorm every night about eleven.*

**road pizza** *n.* a dead animal on the road. ♦ *A bunch of crows were feasting on road pizza when we drove by.*

**road-rash** *n.* an injury from contact with the ground, as in motorcycling or biking. ♦ *Shane picked up a bit of road rash when she fell off her bike.*

**rockhead** *n.* someone who seems to have rocks in the head; a hardheaded or stubborn person. ♦ *What a rockhead! That's a stupid thing to do.*

**rocks 1.** *n.* ice cubes. ♦ *Can I have a few rocks in my drink, please?* **2.** *n.* Xerox Inc. (Securities markets, New York Stock Exchange.) ♦ *When she says, "Buy me a thousand rocks at the market," that means she wants one thousand shares of Xerox at whatever the market price is at the moment.* **3.** *n.* money; a dollar. (Underworld.) ♦ *Twenty rocks for that?* **4.** *n.* the testicles. (Usually objectionable.) ♦ *I was afraid I'd get kicked in the rocks, so I stayed back.*

road pizza: "He says, 'Thank you for the delivery.'"

**rode hard and put away wet** *mod.* misused; ill-used. (Alludes to the mistreatment of a horse.) ♦ *Bad day at the office. I was rode hard and put away wet.*

**roids** *n.* steroids. ♦ *The guy's on roids. He looks like G. I. Joe.*

**roll (a set)** AND **roll a set of prints.** *tv.* to take a set of fingerprints (from someone). ♦ *Danny asked Muggerman to roll a set of prints from the bum and then throw him in the jug.* ♦ *Take him downstairs and roll a set, Sergeant Tartaglia.*

**rony** AND **roni** *n.* pepperoni sausage, as for pizza. ♦ *The geek asked for rony and shrooms, and the counter guy just stared at him.*

**round tripper** *n.* a home run in baseball. ♦ *Ted is responsible for four round trippers in Saturday's game.*

**RSN** *interj.* real soon now. (Used in electronic mail and computer forum or news group messages. Not pronounced aloud.) ♦ *I will post the rest of my trip report RSN.*

**rubber sock** *n.* a timid person; a passive and compliant person. ♦ *Come on! Stand up for your rights. Don't be such a rubber sock!*

**rug rat** AND **ankle biter** *n.* a child. ♦ *Hey, you cute little rug rat, come over here.* ♦ *I got three little ankle biters at home.*

**ruley** *mod.* ideal; excellent. ♦ *Her idea is ruley! She knows what we ought to do!*

**rumble 1.** *in.* to fight. ♦ *The gangs are rumbling over on Fourth Street.* **2.** *n.* a fight; a street fight; a gang fight. ♦ *My brother was hurt in a gang rumble.*

**rump-ranger** *n.* a homosexual male. (Refers to pederasty.) ♦ *A bunch of rump-rangers drifted in just as we drifted out.*

**rundown** *n.* a summary bringing someone up to date. ♦ *Can you give me a rundown on what's happened since noon?*

**runner 1.** *n.* a messenger. ♦ *I work as a runner in the financial district.* **2.** *n.* a person who transports contraband. (Underworld.) ♦ *The runners got away, but we have the goods.*

**run-up** *n.* a movement upward in the value of one or more securities. (Securities markets.) ♦ *The market's had a good run-up in the past week.*

**rush 1.** *n.* a quick print of a day's shooting of a film. (Filmmaking. Usually plural.) ♦ *After today's shooting, we'll watch yesterday's rushes.* **2.** *n.* a period of time when fraternities and sororities are permitted to pursue new members. (Collegiate.) ♦ *When does rush start this year?* **3.** *tv.* [for a fraternity or sorority member] to try to persuade someone to join. ♦ *They can't rush anyone except during rush week.* **4.** *tv.* to court or date someone, usually a woman. (From sense 3.) ♦ *He spent some time trying to rush her but had to give up.* **5.** *n.* a burst of energy or good feeling from a drug; the explosive euphoria of some kinds of drugs. (Drugs.) ♦ *What kind of rush does this have?* **6.** *n.* any excitement; any burst of good feeling. (From sense 5.) ♦ *The wonderful ending to the movie gave me a rush.*

**rusty-dusty** *n.* the posterior; the buttocks. (See also duster.) ♦ *I almost kicked him in the rusty-dusty.*

# S

**sack rat** *n.* someone who spends a lot of time in bed; someone who does not ever seem to get enough sleep. ♦ *Tom is such a sack rat. He can't seem to get enough sleep.*

**sack time 1.** *n.* a period of time spent in bed. ♦ *I need more sack time than most people.* **2.** *n.* time to go to bed. ♦ *Okay, gang, it's sack time. Go home so I can get some sleep!*

**salt horse** *n.* corned or salted beef. ♦ *We made spaghetti sauce with salt horse because that was the only meat we could find.*

**saltine** *n.* a white person. (A play on a kind of salted white cracker [biscuit]. A *cracker* is a derogatory term for a white person.) ♦ *What are those saltines doing in this neighborhood?*

**salty** *n.* expensive; [of a price] falsely bid up. ♦ *That price is a little salty. Is that the best you can do?*

**same o(l)' same o(l)'** AND **SOSO** ['semo(l) 'semo(l)] *n.* the same old thing. ♦ *I'm getting tired of the same ol' same ol'.*

**sand** *n.* sugar. ♦ *Do you use sand in your coffee?*

**sandbag 1.** *tv.* to force someone to do something. ♦ *I don't want to have to sandbag you. Please cooperate.* **2.** *tv.* to deceive someone; to fool someone about one's capabilities. ♦ *Don't let them sandbag you into expecting too little.*

**sauce parlor** *n.* a tavern. ♦ *I wouldn't be caught dead in that sauce parlor.*

**savage** *mod.* excellent. (Collegiate.) ♦ *Man, Fred is a totally savage guy.*

**Say what?** *interrog.* What did you say? ♦ *The old man held his hand to his ear and said, "Say what?"*

**scabbed** ['skæbd] *mod.* cheated in a drug deal; having been sold bogus or inferior drugs. ♦ *Bart got scabbed by a dealer who got arrested the next day.*

**scads** [skædz] *n.* lots (of something). ♦ *I have just scads and scads of paper.*

**scarf 1.** *tv.* to eat something. ♦ *Andy scarfed the whole pie.* **2.** *in.* to eat. ♦ *I'll be with you as soon as I scarf.* **3.** *n.* food. ♦ *I want some good scarf. This stuff stinks.* **4.** *tv.* to steal or **swipe** something. ♦ *The kid scarfed a candy bar, and the store owner called the cops.* **5.** *tv.* to discard something. ♦ *Scarf that thing. It's no good.*

**scarf out** *in.* to overeat. (See also blimp out; pig out.) ♦ *I scarf out every weekend.*

**scarf** sth **down** *tv.* to eat something, perhaps in a hurry; to swallow something, perhaps in a hurry. ♦ *Are you going to scarf this whole thing down?*

**schlemazel** AND **schlemozzle; shlimazl** [ʃləˈmɑzl] *n.* an awkward, bumbling person; a loser. (Yiddish.) ♦ *And* *this poor schlemazel tries to get me to help him paint his fence!*

**schlemiel** AND **schlemihl; shlemiel** [ʃləˈmil] *n.* a gullible person; a loser. (From Hebrew *Shelumiel* via Yiddish.) ♦ *See if you can get that schlemiel to buy the Brooklyn Bridge.*

**schlepper** AND **shlepper** [ˈʃlɛpɚ] *n.* an annoying person who always wants a bargain or a favor. ♦ *Why am I surrounded by people who want something from me? Is this a schlepper colony or what?*

**schloomp** AND **schlump; shlump** [ʃlump OR ʃlʊmp] *n.* a stupid and lazy person. (From German via Yiddish.) ♦ *Tell that schloomp to get busy or get out.*

**schlub** AND **zhlub** [ʃləb OR ʒləb] *n.* a dull, unpolished person, usually a male. (Yiddish.) ♦ *I spent the whole evening listening to that schlub from New Hampshire.*

**schmegegge** AND **schmegeggy** [ʃməˈgegi] **1.** *n.* a stupid person. (Yiddish.) ♦ *Ask the schmegegge standing over by the workbench if he's seen my sky hook.* **2.** *n.* nonsense. ♦ *I've heard enough of your schmegegge. Out!*

**schmendrick** AND **shmendrick** [ˈʃmɛndrɪk] *n.* a stupid and ineffectual nobody. (Yiddish.) ♦ *Some schmendrick from downstairs asked if you could turn down your stereo.*

**schmoozer** *n.* someone who chats or converses well. ♦ *Two old schmoozers sat muttering to one another all afternoon by the duck pond.*

**schmuck** [ʃmək] **1.** *n.* a jerk; a repellent male. (Also a rude term of address. Yiddish.) ♦ *Who is that stupid schmuck over there?* **2.** *n.* a penis. (Yiddish. Usually* objectionable.) ♦ *If I hear that joke about a camel's schmuck one more time, I'm going to scream.*

**schtoonk** AND **shtoonk** [ʃtʊŋk] *n.* a detestable person. (Yiddish.) ♦ *The schtoonk from downstairs was here to talk to you. I told him you died.*

**Schwing!** [ʃʍɪŋ] *exclam.* How exciting!; How stimulating!; Wow! (Originally said on seeing an extremely good-looking or sexually attractive girl. The word is onomatopoetic for the imaginary whishing sound of instant arousal. Many users are not aware of the origins. Potentially offensive.) ♦ *Did you see her? Schwing!*

**scientific wild ass guess** AND **SWAG** *phr. & comp. abb.* a simple guess. (Often objectionable.) ♦ *I don't know at all. That was a SWAG. I always use the SWAG system.*

**Sco 1.** *n.* Frisco; San Francisco. ♦ *If you ever get back to Sco, look me up.* **2.** *imperative* Let's go! ♦ *It's late! Sco!*

**scooters** [ˈskutɚz] *mod.* crazy; confused. ♦ *It's days like this that make me think I'm scooters.*

**scope (on)** so *tv. & in.* to evaluate a member of the opposite sex visually. ♦ *He scoped every girl who came in the door.*

**scrambled eggs** *n.* rank insignia on a military officer's uniform. ♦ *I know his rank is high because of the "scrambled eggs," but I don't know how high.*

**scratch 1.** *n.* money. ♦ *I just don't have the scratch.* **2.** *tv.* to eliminate something from a list; to cancel something. ♦ *We decided to scratch the idea of a new car. The old one will have to do.* **3.** *mod.* impromptu; temporary. ♦ *We started a scratch game of basketball, but most of the girls had to leave at dinnertime.*

**screw** SO **over** *tv.* to give someone a very bad time; to scold someone severely. ♦ *Let's get those kids in here and screw over every one of them. This stuff can't continue.*

**screwage** *n.* copulation; acts of copulation; the people and actions of copulation. ♦ *His mind is on nothing but "screwage" and how to get some of it.*

**screwed 1.** *mod.* copulated with. (Usually objectionable.) ♦ *I got myself good and screwed, and I haven't felt better in months.* **2.** *mod.* cheated. ♦ *Wow, you got screwed on that watch.* **3.** AND **screwed tight** *mod.* alcohol intoxicated. ♦ *She's not just drunk; she's screwed tight.* **4.** *mod.* bested; defeated; cheated. ♦ *I really got screwed at the garage.*

**script(t)** *n.* a note; any piece of paper with a written message. (Underworld.) ♦ *Make him sign this script before you let him in on the deal.*

**scrog** [skrɔg] *tv. & in.* to have sex; to copulate [with] someone. (Usually objectionable.) ♦ *You know what! I think those people over in the corner are scrogging!*

**scronched** [skrɔntʃt] *mod.* alcohol intoxicated. ♦ *She just sat there and got scronched.*

**scrud** *n.* a serious disease; a sexually transmitted disease. (Military.) ♦ *Poor dumb Charlie can't tell scrud from crotch rot.*

**scrump** [skrəmp] *tv. & in.* to copulate [with] someone. (Usually objectionable.) ♦ *The movie showed a scene of some woman scrumping her lover.*

**scrunch** [skrəntʃ] *tv.* to crush or crunch. ♦ *I hate crowds. I am afraid people will scrunch me.*

**scrunge** [skrʌndʒ] *n.* nastiness; gunk. ♦ *What is this scrunge on my shoe?*

**scupper up** *in.* to drink liquor, especially beer. ♦ *Tom goes home to scupper up every evening.*

**scut** [skʌt] *n.* a despicable person. (Teens and collegiate.) ♦ *It's scuts like that who give all us really rad kids a bad name.*

**scuzzo** *n.* a repellent person. ♦ *There's the scuzzo who thinks I like him.*

**scuzzy** ['skʌzi] *mod.* repellent; unkempt. ♦ *His clothes are always so scuzzy. He probably keeps them in a pile in his room.*

**seam-squirrels** *n.* lice. (See also **pants rabbits**. Contrived.) ♦ *I got an itch. Must be seam-squirrels.*

**seegar** ['sigɑr] *n.* a cigar. (Folksy. The stress is on the first syllable.) ♦ *There's nothing like a fine seegar after a nice bowl of hot chili.*

**self-propelled sandbag** *n.* a U.S. Marine. (Persian Gulf War.) ♦ *Those guys are just self-propelled sandbags. They are fearless.*

**send** so **to glory 1.** *tv.* to kill someone. ♦ *One shot sent him to glory.* **2.** *tv.* to officiate at the burial services for someone. ♦ *The preacher sent him to glory amidst the sobs of six or seven former fans.*

**senior moment** *n.* a lapse of memory in an older person. ♦ *I had a senior moment and forgot your name. Sorry.*

**serious** *mod.* good; profound; excellent. ♦ *Man, these tunes are, like, serious.*

**seven-seven-three-aitch** AND **773H** *n.* hell. (This is based on the printed word *HELL* rotated 180 degrees. Jocular.) ♦ *What the seven-seven-three-aitch is going on around here?*

**sewer hog** *n.* a ditch digger; a sewer worker. ♦ *A sewer hog doesn't get a lot of chances to pal around with the gentry, but the pay's plenty good.*

**sewermouth** *n.* someone who uses vile language constantly. (Also a rude term of address.) ♦ *If you're going to be a sewermouth, I wish you would leave.*

**shades** *n.* dark glasses. ♦ *Where are my shades? The sun is too bright.*

**shagged** *mod.* alcohol intoxicated. ♦ *Nobody is not too shagged to drive—or something like that.*

**shakedown** *n.* an act of extortion. (Underworld.) ♦ *Mary was giving Bruno the shakedown, so he tried to put her out of the way.*

**shaky-cam** *n.* a camera, used mainly in advertisements and documentaries, that is shaken and moved constantly to create a sense of excitement, urgency, or crisis. ♦ *We can't afford much in the way of costumes for the sequence, so we will use the shaky-cam and shoot it in dim light.*

**shammered** *mod.* drunk. ♦ *The guys went out and really got shammered.*

**shank 1.** *n.* a knife; a homemade knife. (Possibly named for a bone handle.) ♦ *The mugger pulled a shank on the victim.* **2.** *in.* to dance. (This *shank* refers to a leg bone.) ♦ *They were busy shankin' and didn't hear the gunshots.*

**shark 1.** *n.* a swindler; a confidence operator. (Underworld.) ♦ *The sharks were lined up ten deep to get at the blue-eyed new owner of the bowling alley.* **2.** *n.* a lawyer. (Derogatory.) ♦ *Some shark is trying to squeeze a few grand out of me.*

**shark repellent** *n.* something that prevents corporate takeovers. (Securities markets.) ♦ *Acme Systems tried again to get its board to approve a shark repellent to keep the Widget cartel from acquiring it.*

**Shazzam!** [ʃəˈzæm] *exclam.* Wow!; Would you believe? (An incantation used by the comic book character Captain Marvel.) ♦ *And there was my ring—Shazzam!— right on the sidewalk!* ♦ *Shazzam! I passed the test!*

**sheen** [ʃin] *n.* a car. (From *machine*.) ♦ *You have one fine sheen there.*

**Sheesh!** [ʃiʃ] *exclam.* Damn!; Shit! (A euphemism for Shit!) ♦ *Sheesh! What a mess!*

**sheisty** *mod.* unscrupulous in the manner of a shyster lawyer. ♦ *What a sheisty thing to do! Can't trust anybody!*

**shekels** [ˈʃɛkl̩z] *n.* dollars; money. (From the Hebrew name for a unit of weight.) ♦ *You got a few shekels you can spare?*

**shit 1.** *n.* dung; feces. (Usually objectionable. Colloquial. Objectionable for many people.) ♦ *Gee! I stepped in some shit!* **2.** *in.* to defecate. (Usually objectionable.) ♦ *This dog needs to shit. Take it for a walk.* **3.** *n.* any trash or unwanted material; junk; clutter. (Usually objectionable.) ♦ *Clean up this shit and don't let this place get so messy.* **4.** *n.* a wretched person; a despised person.

(Rude and derogatory.) ♦ *You stupid shit! Look what you did!* **5.** *n.* one's personal belongings. (Usually objectionable.) ♦ *I gotta get my shit from the kitchen and get outa here.* **6.** *n.* lies; nonsense. (From **bullshit.** Usually objectionable.) ♦ *All I ever hear out of you is shit.* **7.** *tv.* to deceive someone; to lie to someone. ♦ *Stop shittin' me, you bastard!* **8.** *n.* drugs, especially heroin or marijuana. (Usually objectionable.) ♦ *You are going to have to get off this shit or you're gonna die.* **9.** *exclam.* a general expression of disgust. (Usually **Shit!** Usually objectionable.) ♦ *Oh, shit! What a mess!*

**shit a brick** *tv.* to be very upset; to be extremely angry. (Usually objectionable.) ♦ *I was so mad, I almost shit a brick!*

**Shit happens.** *interj.* Bad things just happen. (Usually objectionable.) ♦ *Shit happens. There's nothing that can be done about it.*

**shit on a shingle** *n.* creamed chipped beef on toast. (Military. Usually objectionable.) ♦ *Oh, no, it's shit on a shingle again tonight.*

**shitsky** ['ʃɪtski] **1.** *n.* dung. (Usually objectionable.) ♦ *Some rude dog has left a little pile of grade-A shitsky on the sidewalk.* **2.** *n.* a despicable person. (Rude and derogatory.) ♦ *With a shitsky like that on your side, who needs enemies?*

**shiv** AND **chiv** [ʃɪv] **1.** *n.* a knife. (Underworld.) ♦ *Swiftly and silently his shiv found its way up under Rocko's ribs. All for a silly dame.* **2.** *tv.* to stab someone. (Underworld.) ♦ *The boss told Joel Cairo to get Sam one way or the other—shiv him, burn him, clobber him—but get him.*

**shmen** [ʃmɛn] *n.* freshmen. ♦ *A couple of shmen wandered by—looking sort of lost.* ♦ *The shmen are having a party all to themselves this Friday.*

**shoot** oneself **in the foot** *tv.* to cause oneself difficulty; to be the author of one's own doom. ♦ *Again, he shot himself in the foot with his open and honest dealings with the press.*

**shot in the neck 1.** *n.* a drink of straight whiskey. ♦ *Willy took a little shot in the neck before heading out into the cold.* **2.** *mod.* alcohol intoxicated. ♦ *What's wrong with Harry is that he's shot in the neck every day by supper.*

**shot to the curb** *mod.* without money or a place to live; living in the gutter; down and out. (Alluding to being on the streets.) ♦ *I'm totally out of bills, man. Shot to the curb.*

**shotty back** *n.* the seat in a car behind the shotgun or passenger seat. ♦ *I wanna ride shotty back!*

**shout** *n.* an exclamation point. ♦ *Put a shout at the end of the line. Make this dull story more sexy.*

**shower scum** *n.* a despised person; despised people. (See also **bathtub scum; pond scum.**) ♦ *Who is the shower scum who put a cigarette butt in my houseplant?*

**shrapnel** *n.* a few small coins left as a tip. ♦ *He just toked me a few bits of schrapnel!*

**shriek** *n.* an exclamation point. ♦ *Take off that shriek. You use too many of those things.*

**shrooms** [ʃrumz] **1.** *n.* the tips of the peyote cactus that contain mescaline. (Drugs. From *mushrooms*. Not really a mushroom.) ♦ *I got some shrooms. Ya wanna come over?* **2.** *n.* mushrooms. (From sense 1.) ♦ *Do you want shrooms on your pizza?*

**shuck** [ʃək] **1.** *n.* an insincere person. ♦ *The guy's a shuck. Don't believe a thing he says!* **2.** *tv. & in.* to kid someone; to tease someone. ♦ *Cool it! I'm just shucking.* **3.** *tv.* to swindle someone; to deceive someone. ♦ *He was going to shuck the mayor, but people were beginning to talk, so he blew town.* **4.** *n.* a hoax. ♦ *How could you fall for that old shuck?* **5.** AND **shuck down** *tv. & in.* to undress oneself; to remove one's clothing. ♦ *He shucked down and showered and was at work in twenty minutes.*

**shutters** *n.* the eyelids. ♦ *She blinked those yummy shutters over those bedroom eyes, and my knees turned to mush.*

**shwench** [ʃmɛntʃ] *n.* a female freshman. (Collegiate. From *fresh* + *wench*.) ♦ *A couple of giggling shwenches showed up to cheer on the team.*

**signify 1.** *in.* to cause trouble for fun; to stir things up. (Black.) ♦ *What are all these cats signifying about anyway?* **2.** *in.* to try to look more important than one really is; to brag; to **strut** one's **stuff.** (Black.) ♦ *See that dude signify like somebody important?*

**silks** *n.* clothing. ♦ *I gotta get some new silks before spring.*

**silo drippings** *n.* alcohol allegedly obtained at the base of a silo containing fermenting corn. ♦ *The old-timer called his moonshine "silo drippings."*

**simoleon** [sɪ'molɪən] *n.* a dollar. (Underworld.) ♦ *For only one simoleon, you get a ticket to the greatest show on earth.*

**sink** *tv.* to swallow some food or drink. ♦ *Larry stopped at a tavern to sink a short one.*

**sipster** *n.* a tippler; a drunkard. ♦ *The old lady is a sipster who says she drinks a little wine to help her arthritis.*

**sitch** *n.* situation. (Streets.) ♦ *You in one bad sitch, bitch!*

**sixer** *n.* a six-pack beverage container. (Usually refers to beer.) ♦ *Tom showed up with three sixers and a bushel of pretzels, and we all watched the game together.*

**skag jones** AND **scag jones** *n.* an addiction to heroin. (Drugs. Here *jones* is a "thing" = craving.) ♦ *She has a serious skag jones.*

**skank** AND **scank** [skæŋk] **1.** *n.* an ugly (young) woman. (Collegiate.) ♦ *What a skank she is! Give her a comb or something.* **2.** *in.* to appear ugly. ♦ *Both sisters skank. Must be hereditary.*

**skanky** ['skæŋki] *mod.* ugly; repellent, usually said of a woman. (Collegiate.) ♦ *She is so skanky! That grody hairdo doesn't help either.*

**skeet-shooting** *n.* the act of blowing one's nose by pinching one nostril and using no tissue or handkerchief. ♦ *There is nothing more disgusting than a bunch of college boys belching and skeet-shooting.*

**sketchy** *mod.* unsafe; illegal; risky. (Alluding to danger due to lack of knowledge.) ♦ *Why are we going down in that sketchy place on this silly errand?*

**skid-lid** *n.* a motorcycle helmet. ♦ *The law has no business telling me I gotta wear a skid-lid.*

**skillion** ['skɪljən] *n.* an imaginary enormous number. ♦ *I have a skillion reasons why I won't marry you.*

**sko 1.** AND **sgo** ['sko AND 'sgo] *in.* Let's go. (Now considered current slang even though it has been informal colloquial for decades.) ♦ *It's time to hit the road. Sgo.* **2.** *n.* a skanky hoe. ♦ *What a sko, fo sho!*

**skrilla** AND **skrill** *n.* money. ♦ *I'm totally outa skrilla, man. Shot to the curb.*

**skurf** [skɚf] *in.* to skateboard. (From the words *skate* and *surf.*) ♦ *He skurfed from city hall to the post office.*

**sky** *in.* to travel (to somewhere) in an airplane. ♦ *I decided to sky down to Orlando for the weekend.*

**sky rug** *n.* a toupee; a man's wig. ♦ *I think he is wearing a sky rug.*

**slackmaster** *n.* someone who slacks off a lot; someone who doesn't work hard enough or at all. ♦ *He never does his share. Nothing but a slackmaster!*

**slamming** *mod.* great. ♦ *We had one slamming time last night.*

**slave market** *n.* a job market where many candidates for jobs come face to face with potential employers. ♦ *I gotta go to the annual slave market this year. We're hiring for a change.*

**sleeper 1.** *n.* a sleeping pill. ♦ *She took a handful of sleepers with a glass of booze, and that was it.* **2.** *n.* someone or something that achieves fame after a period of invisibility. ♦ *The movie "Red Willow" was undoubtedly the sleeper of the year, winning six awards.*

**sleepfest** *n.* something, such as a dull lecture, that induces a long period of sleep. ♦ *The history lecture today was a real sleepfest.*

**slip so five** *tv.* to shake someone's hand. ♦ *Billy slipped me five, and we sat down to discuss old times.*

**slob up** *in.* to eat. ♦ *Fred stopped slobbing up long enough to change the channel on the TV set.*

**sludgeball** ['sləʤbɑl] *n.* a despicable and repellent person. ♦ *Mike is such a sludgeball! Why do you keep seeing him?*

**slugged** *mod.* alcohol intoxicated. ♦ *I'm slugged—skunked, you know, corned. And I think I am going to sick up.* ♦ *Ted realized that he was slugged out of his mind, but tried to get the bartender to serve him another drink.*

**slummy** ['sləmi] *mod.* lousy. ♦ *This place is not slummy!*

**small change** *n.* an insignificant person. (Also a rude term of address.) ♦ *The guy you think is small change happens to own this building you seem to be guarding so well.*

**smarts** *n.* intelligence. ♦ *I got the smarts to do the job. All I need is someone to trust me.*

**smash** *n.* wine. (Streets. Because it is made from smashed grapes.) ♦ *I got a bottle of smash in my car.*

**smeg 1.** *n.* smegma. ♦ *Smeg sounds completely disgusting.* **2.** *n.* a nasty thing, substance, or person. (Also a term of address.) ♦ *Get out of here, you smeg.*

**smell it up** AND **smell the stuff** *tv.* to sniff or snort powdered drugs, usually cocaine. (Drugs.) ♦ *One of those guys shoots it; the other smells it up.* ♦ *The addict put the powder in a narrow row in order to "smell the stuff."*

snail-mail

**smeller** *n.* (one's) nose. ♦ *I think my smeller's gone bad because of my cold.*

**smoke both ends of the cigar** *tv.* to perform male to male fellatio. ♦ *I think they're smoking both ends of the cigar.*

**smokin'** ['smokən] *mod.* excellent; really hot; overpowering. ♦ *If you wanna hear some smokin' vinyl, just stay tuned.*

**smurfed** [sməft] *mod.* having to do with a bank that has been used to **launder** money. ♦ *The teller came slowly into the office. "I think we were smurfed," she said.*

**snail-mail** *n.* post office mail; regular mail as opposed to electronic mail. (Refers to the slowness of regular mail in comparison to electronic mail or faxes.) ♦ *There are lots of color pictures in the article, so I will send you the original by snail-mail.*

**snake 1.** *in.* to scheme; to plot and plan. (Prisons.) ♦ *He spent a lot of time snaking about that job.* **2.** *tv.* to steal something. ♦ *Where did you snake that bike?*

**snapper** *n.* a strange person. ♦ *Willy is sort of a snapper, but he's a nice guy.*

**snappers** *n.* the teeth. (Folksy.) ♦ *I couldn't talk to you on the phone till I got my snappers in.*

**sneak** *n.* a sneak preview of a movie. ♦ *There was a good sneak at the Granada last night.*

**sneaks** *n.* sneakers. ♦ *She wore red sneaks and a mini.*

**snipe** *n.* a cigarette or cigar butt. ♦ *Down on skid row, a snipe won't be on the sidewalk for ten seconds.*

**snork** [snork] *in.* to smoke marijuana or hashish. (Drugs.) ♦ *They snorked until they could snork no more.*

**snow bunny 1.** *n.* someone learning to ski. ♦ *Most of the snow bunnies come here to socialize.* **2.** *n.* a female skier. ♦ *This place is swarming with snow bunnies who have never even seen a ski.* **3.** *n.* a cocaine user. ♦ *How can these suburban snow bunnies afford such big habits?*

**snozzled** ['snɑzl̩d] *mod.* alcohol intoxicated. ♦ *How can anybody be so snozzled on four beers?*

**snuff it** *tv.* to die. ♦ *The cat leapt straight up in the air and snuffed it.*

**so last year** *n.* outdated. ♦ *That outfit is so last year!*

**so or sth from hell** *n.* someone or something very intense, annoying, or challenging. (As if the person or thing were a demon from hell.) ♦ *I just came back from a cruise* *from hell and have lots of horror stories to tell about the trip.*

**so's ass is grass** *phr.* Someone has had it.; It is the end for someone. (Usually objectionable.) ♦ *You do that again, and your ass is grass!*

**soak** one's **face** *tv.* to drink heavily. ♦ *They're down at the tavern soaking their faces.*

**sofa spud** ['sofə 'spəd] *n.* someone who spends a great deal of time sitting and watching television. (A play on **couch potato**.) ♦ *Sofa spuds have been getting a lot of attention in the newspapers.*

**software rot** *n.* an imaginary disease that causes computer programs to go bad over a long period of time. (Computers.) ♦ *What you have here is not a bug, but just plain old software rot.*

**sold cober** ['sold 'kobɚ] *mod.* sober. (A deliberate spoonerism on **cold sober**. Similar to **jober as a sudge**.) ♦ *What do you mean drunk? Why, I'm sold cober.*

**soph** [sɑf] *n.* a sophomore. ♦ *He's just a soph, so he still might grow a little.*

**sorry-ass(ed) 1.** *mod.* sad and depressed. (Usually objectionable.) ♦ *Man, old Charlie was about the most sorry-ass dude you ever saw.* **2.** *mod.* worthless; poor quality. (Usually objectionable.) ♦ *How much longer do I have to drive this sorry-ass excuse for an automobile?*

**sosh** [sɑʃ] *n.* a (young female) socialite. ♦ *Tiffany looks like a sosh, but she's just a working girl.*

**sounds** *n.* music; records. ♦ *I got some new sounds. Ya wanna come over and listen?*

**soup sandwich** *n.* something impossibly messy or impossible to deal with. ♦ *This whole project is just a soup sandwich. I'll never get it straightened out.*

**soup-strainer** *n.* a mustache. ♦ *Jerry had a big bushy soup-strainer that he was very proud of.*

**southern-fried** *mod.* alcohol intoxicated. (An elaboration of fried, referring to *fried chicken*.) ♦ *When Bob came home southern-fried, his wife nearly killed him.*

**spam 1.** *n.* something disliked, typically, but not necessarily, food. (From the brand name of a canned meat product.) ♦ *I can't eat this "spam." It could be spoiled.* **2.** *n.* one or a series of uninvited e-mail messages advertising money-making schemes, pornography, or sales of any kind. ♦ *If I don't recognize the sender, I assume the message is spam and I delete it.* **3.** *tv.* to clutter or fill someone's e-mail account with spam (sense 2). ♦ *Some jerk is spamming me with an advertisement for dirty pictures.*

**sparkler** *n.* a diamond; gemstones. ♦ *Look at the sparklers on that old dame.*

**spaz around** *in.* to waste time; to mess around. ♦ *You kids are always spazzing around. Why don't you get a job?*

**Speak it!** *exclam.* Say it!; You said it!; That's telling them! ♦ *Speak it, girlfriend! Tell him off!*

**speedo 1.** *n.* a speedometer. ♦ *I think my speedo is broken. It says we're standing still.* **2.** a tight-fitting swim brief, usually revealing. (From the protected trade name of the swimming suit manufacturer.) ♦ *You can't go out in public wearing that speedo! I can see everything!*

**spendy** *mod.* expensive; pricey. *That brand is a little spendy, but the difference may be worth it.*

**spiff** *n.* extra money paid to a salesperson to sell certain merchandise aggressively. (See also push money.) ♦ *The manufacturer supplied a little spiff that even the store manager didn't know about.*

**spill** *in.* to confess. (Underworld.) ♦ *The cops tried to get her to spill, but she just sat there.*

**spinach** *n.* money. (Because it is green.) ♦ *Look at this! One hundred dollars in good old American spinach!*

**spinner** *n.* a bullet. ♦ *Harry the Horse's shot sent a spinner into Lefty's gut.*

**splooge** AND **spooge** **1.** *n.* semen. ♦ *Clean up that splooge before somebody sees it!* **2.** *in.* to ejaculate. ♦ *I almost splooged when I saw her bend over.*

**spokes** *n.* lists of jokes, sent from friends via e-mail; joke spam. ♦ *I don't know what's worse, spokes or spam.*

**spoofing** AND **carding; phishing** **1.** *n.* stealing passwords and personal information on the Internet. (See also phish for an explanation.) ♦ *He set up an evil twin for spoofing at the coffee shop.*

**spot market** *n.* the open market where deals are made on the spot. (Securities markets.) ♦ *Oil reached nearly fifty-five dollars a barrel on the spot market.*

**sprout** *n.* a child. ♦ *A little sprout came up and tried to sell me a ticket to a game.*

**sprout wings** **1.** *tv.* to die and become an angel. ♦ *I'm not ready to sprout wings yet. I've got a few more years.* **2.** *tv.* to be so good as to become an angel. ♦ *The kid is* *not about to sprout wings, but he probably won't get into jail again.*

**spyware** AND **data miner** *n.* a kind of malicious software that gathers private information from a personal computer and sends it to another computer. ♦ *I have a little program that roots out spyware from my computer.* ♦ *It found a data miner lurking among my digital images.*

**square biscuit** *n.* a plain, drab, and dull person. ♦ *Old Roger is a square biscuit and acts like a school marm.*

**square john broad** *n.* an honest, straightforward woman. (Underworld.) ♦ *We need a square john broad to give this place a look of respectability.*

**squib** [skmɪb] *n.* a notice; a small advertisement. ♦ *There was a squib in the paper about your project.*

**squid** [skmɪd] *n.* an earnest student; a collegiate wimp. (Collegiate. Refers to sliminess.) ♦ *This whole campus is populated by squids and nerds.*

**squiggle** ['skmɪgl] *n.* a wiggly mark. ♦ *That squiggle is my signature.*

**squirrel 1.** *n.* a strange or eccentric person. ♦ *Martin can be such a squirrel.* **2.** *n.* a car engine's horsepower. (Usually plural.) ♦ *I got 440 squirrels and a gaggle of carburetors.*

**squirrel-food** *n.* a nut; a loony person. ♦ *The driver of the car—squirrel-food, for sure—just sat there smiling.* ♦ *Some squirrel-food came over and asked for a sky hook.*

**squooshy** ['skmʊʃi AND 'skmuʃi] *mod.* soft; squishy. ♦ *I like to walk barefooted in squooshy mud.*

**stallion** *n.* a tall, good-looking woman. ♦ *Dana is really a stallion!*

**standee** *n.* someone who must stand (at some event). ♦ *Can I get in as a standee, or do I have to wait for the next showing?*

**stanza** ['stænzə] *n.* an inning in baseball or some other division of a ball game. ♦ *He's doing better than he was in the last stanza.*

**static** *n.* complaints. ♦ *I don't expect any static because of the noise. I warned the neighbors about the party.*

**steam** so's **beam** *tv.* to make someone angry. ♦ *Come on, don't steam your beam. Remember how hard times are now.*

**steamroller** *tv.* to force something to be approved; to force something to happen. ♦ *He plans to steamroller this bill through Congress, but it just won't work.*

**steelo** *n.* style. ♦ *What you lack is steelo! Style! Class! You are dull!*

**steenth** [stintθ] *n.* one *sixteenth,* used in quoting securities prices. (Securities markets.) ♦ *This issue was up only a few steenths for the whole week.*

**stellar** ['stɛlɚ] *mod.* excellent; grand. ♦ *Ronald Simpson gave us a stellar characterization of Boris, but the chorus was a disappointment.*

**step off the curb** *in.* to die. (Alludes to stepping out in front of a vehicle that causes one's death.) ♦ *Ralph almost stepped off the curb during his operation.*

sticker shock

**stern** *n.* the posterior; buttocks. ♦ *The little airplane crashed right into the stern of an enormous lady who didn't even notice.*

**sticker shock** *n.* the shock at seeing just how much something new, usually an automobile, costs as determined by looking at the price tag or sticker. ♦ *I went to a car dealer today, and I am still suffering from sticker shock.*

**stinger** *n.* the drawback; the catch; the hitch. ♦ *Sounds good, but what's the stinger?*

**stink on ice** *in.* to be really rotten, bad, poorly done, or repellent. (So rotten as to reek even when frozen.) ♦ *This show stinks on ice.*

**stinking rich** *mod.* very rich. ♦ *I'd like to be stinking rich for the rest of my life.*

**stone groove** *n.* something really **cool**; a fine party or concert. ♦ *This affair is not what I would call a stone groove. Stone beige, maybe.*

**stoned out of** one's **squash** *mod.* alcohol or drug intoxicated. ♦ *Britney will drink a little now and then, but she never gets stoned out of her squash.*

**stones 1.** *n.* the testicles. (Also a Standard English euphemism. See also **rocks**.) ♦ *He got hit in the stones.* **2.** *mod.* courage; bravado. ♦ *Come on, Willy, show some stones!*

**stonkered** ['stɔŋkɚd] **1.** *mod.* killed. ♦ *The car crashed into him and he was stonkered for sure.* **2.** *mod.* alcohol intoxicated. ♦ *My buddy here is stonkered and needs a ride, and can I have one, too?*

**storked** *mod.* pregnant. ♦ *She got herself good and storked. Now what?*

**str8** *mod.* straight. ♦ *Now tell it to me str8!*

**straight low** *n.* the absolute truth; the true **lowdown**. (Prisons.) ♦ *Nobody ain't gonna tell no warden the straight low; you can be sure of that.*

**straight up 1.** *mod.* [of someone] upright and honest. ♦ *A fine guy—really straight up.* ♦ *She is one of the most straight up brokers in town.* **2.** *mod.* without ice; neat. ♦ *I'll have a bourbon, straight up, please.* **3.** *mod.* sunnyside up; having to do with eggs cooked with yellow yolks facing straight up. ♦ *I like my eggs straight up, but the white part has to be cooked solid.*

**strap** *n.* an athlete, not necessarily male. (From jockstrap.) ♦ *The guy's a strap all right, but he's not dumb.*

**street cred** *n.* credibility on the streets. (Streets.) ♦ *If I drove a ride like that, I'd lose my street cred.*

**street people** *n.* people who live in the streets; homeless people. ♦ *There are a lot of cold street people at this time of the year.*

**street smart** *mod.* wise in the ways of urban life; wise in the ways of tough neighborhoods. ♦ *Bess wasn't street smart enough to survive by herself.*

**street smarts** *n.* the knowledge and ability to survive on the urban street. ♦ *If you don't have street smarts, you won't last long out there.*

**street sweeper** *n.* a machine gun. ♦ *In my neighborhood, the sound of street sweepers is about as common as the sound of horns honking.*

**streeter** *n.* an urban street person. ♦ *These streeters have to be bright and clever just to survive.*

**strung-out shape** *n.* a tired and exhausted condition. ♦ *They were sort of in strung-out shape, tired and ready for the sack.*

**strunk** *mod.* stoned and drunk. (Contrived.) ♦ *He's too strunk to stand up.*

**stubby** *mod.* cool; good-looking. ♦ *Man, you're stubby. Nice kicks!*

**studly** *mod.* a virile and attractive male. ♦ *I had no idea you were going to bring along such a studly guy!*

**stud-muffin** *n.* a really good-looking guy; a stud. ♦ *Who's the stud-muffin with Sally?*

**study animal** *n.* someone who studies hard. (A play on party animal.) ♦ *At the end of the school year every party animal turns into a study animal.*

**stumper** *n.* a shoe. (Streets. Usually plural.) ♦ *Make those stumpers shine!*

**stumps** *n.* a person's legs. ♦ *You need good strong stumps to do that kind of climbing.*

**stunting** *mod.* well dressed. ♦ *Mooshoo is iced out and stunting!*

**stupehead** *n.* a stupid person; a blockhead. (Also a term of address.) ♦ *What a stupehead!*

**submarine 1.** AND **sub; hoagy; torpedo; grinder; poor boy; hero** *n.* a long sandwich containing many different foods. (Sometimes many feet long. It is cut into smaller segments for serving a group. Usually contains sliced meats and cheese, as well as tomatoes and onions. Terms vary depending on where you are in the country.) ♦ *He ordered a submarine, but he couldn't finish it.* **2.** *n.* a large marijuana cigarette. ♦ *Look at the size of that sub!* **3.** *n.* [menstrual] tampon. ♦ *My God! I'm out of submarines!*

**suck face** *tv.* to kiss. ♦ *The kid said he was going out to suck face. It sounds awful.*

**suckabuck** *mod.* greedy; exhibiting greed. ♦ *She is such a suckabuck landlady that it makes me want to move.*

**sucker 1.** AND **sucka** *n.* a dupe; an easy mark. ♦ *See if you can sell that sucker the Brooklyn Bridge.* **2.** *tv.* to trick or victimize someone. ♦ *That crook suckered me. I should have known better.* **3.** *n.* an annoying person. (Also a rude term of address.) ♦ *I am really sick of that* *sucker hanging around here.* **4.** *n.* a gadget; a thing. ♦ *Now, you put this little sucker right into this slot.*

**superfly** *mod.* excellent; wonderful. ♦ *I don't care about this superfly gent of yours. If he doesn't have a job, I don't want you seeing him anymore. Ya hear?*

**super-strap** *n.* an earnest and hardworking student. ♦ *I couldn't be a super-strap even if I had the brains. I just don't care that much.*

**surf the net** *tv.* to browse through the offerings of the Internet. ♦ *He surfs the net for three hours each evening.*

**suss** so **out** ['sǝs...] *tv.* to try to figure someone out. ♦ *I can't seem to suss Tom out. What a strange guy.*

**Suzy** *n.* a U.S. one-dollar coin bearing a likeness of Susan B. Anthony. ♦ *I've got two Suzies I want to get rid of.*

**swamped 1.** *mod.* very, very busy. ♦ *I can't handle it now. I'm swamped.* **2.** *mod.* alcohol intoxicated. ♦ *Look at him! He's swamped—stoned out of his mind.*

**sweat bullets** *tv.* to suffer about something; to be anxious or nervous about something; to **sweat blood.** ♦ *The kid sat in the waiting room, sweating bullets while the surgeons worked on his brother.*

**sweat sock** *n.* an athlete; a jock. (Usually plural.) ♦ *I live in a dorm with a bunch of sweat socks. They feed us well, anyway.*

**sweetener** *n.* extra encouragement, usually in the form of money. ♦ *Money makes the best sweetener around.*

**swellelegant** ['swɛl'ɛlǝgǝnt] *mod.* really fine. (From *swell* and *elegant.*) ♦ *Gee, this place is sure swellelegant!*

**swigged** AND **swiggled** [swɪgd AND ˈswɪgl̩d] *mod.* alcohol intoxicated; tipsy. ♦ *Man, is she ever swigged!*

**swill-up** *n.* a drinking bout. ♦ *There was a swill-up at the frat house last week.*

**swindle sheet** *n.* an expense account record sheet or book. ♦ *I turned in my swindle sheet yesterday, and no one challenged the $400 for new shoes.*

**switch** *n.* a switchblade knife. (The folding pocket knife springs open when a button is pushed.) ♦ *They found a switch in his pocket when they searched him.*

**switch-hitter 1.** *n.* a ballplayer who bats either right-handed or left-handed. (Baseball.) ♦ *I'm not a switch-hitter. In fact, I can hardly hit the ball at all.* **2.** *n.* a bisexual person. (From sense 1.) ♦ *Bart finally decided he was a switch-hitter and asked Brad for a date since Mary was busy.*

**swizzle-stick** *n.* a drunkard. (From the name of a short stick used to stir an alcoholic drink.) ♦ *That guy is a swizzle-stick. Don't give him any more.*

**sword swallowing** *n.* fellatio. ♦ *The headmaster caught him in an act of sword swallowing.*

# T

**tabbed** *mod.* well-dressed. (Streets.) ♦ *She's really tabbed in some nice threads.*

**table-hop** *in.* to move from table to table in a restaurant, nightclub, bar, etc. ♦ *They would table-hop—to the great dismay of the waiters.*

**tagger** *n.* a gang member who puts gang signs and themes on things with spray paint. ♦ *Sam is our best tagger. Man, he's an artist.*

**take a bath (on** sth**)** *tv.* to have large financial losses on an investment. ♦ *The broker warned me that I might take a bath if I bought this stuff.*

**take a chill pill** *tv.* to calm down; to relax. ♦ *The police officer told Jim to take a chill pill and answer the questions.*

**take a dirt nap** *tv.* to die and be buried. ♦ *I don't want to end up taking a dirt nap during this operation.*

**take a whack at** so/sth *tv.* to hit at someone or something. ♦ *Jerry got an ax and took a whack at the tree but didn't do much damage.*

**take a whack at** sth *tv.* to have a try at something. ♦ *Why don't you practice a little while and take a whack at it tomorrow?*

take a bath (on sth): "You might take a bath on this investment."

**take care of number one** AND **take care of numero uno** *tv.* to take care of oneself. (See also numero uno.) ♦ *Arthur, like everybody else, is most concerned with taking care of number one.*

**Take it down a thou(sand)!** *in.* Cool down!; Calm down!; Quiet down! ♦ *You are wild! Take it down a thou and let's try again to talk this out.*

**take it to the street** *tv.* to tell everyone about your problems. ♦ *If there's something bothering her, she's gonna take it to the street, first thing.*

**take names** *tv.* to make a list of wrongdoers. (Often figuratively, as with a schoolteacher, whose major weapon is to take names and send them to the principal.) ♦ *The boss is madder than hell, and he's taking names.*

**take on fuel** *tv.* to drink alcohol to excess. ♦ *They stopped at the tavern to take on fuel.*

**take pictures** *tv.* for a highway patrol officer to use radar. (Citizens band radio.) ◆ *There's a smokey under the bridge taking pictures.*

**take** so **out 1.** *tv.* to block someone, as in a football game. ◆ *I was supposed to take the left end out, but I was trapped under the center.* **2.** *tv.* to kill someone. (Underworld.) ◆ *The boss told Rocko to take out Marlowe.* **3.** *tv.* to date someone. ◆ *She wanted to take him out for an evening.*

**take** sth **public 1.** *tv.* to make something known to the public. ◆ *You gotta take it public—put it on the street—even when it's none of your business.* ◆ *Don't take it public. You'll just get talked about.* **2.** *tv.* to sell shares in a company to the general public. (Securities markets.) ◆ *We're going to take it public whenever the market looks good.*

**take the fifth 1.** AND **five it** *tv.* to refuse to testify to a U.S. legislative committee under the protection of the Fifth Amendment to the U.S. Constitution. ◆ *The lawyer just sat there and said, "Five it" after every question.* **2.** *tv.* to decline to answer any questions. ◆ *I'll take the fifth on that one. Ask Fred.*

**take the piss out of** so *tv.* to humble someone; to make someone—usually a male—less cocky, perhaps by violence. (Usually objectionable.) ◆ *You need somebody to take the piss outa you!*

**take the spear (in** one's **chest)** *tv.* to accept full blame for something; to accept the full brunt of the punishment for something. ◆ *The admiral got the short straw and had to take the spear in his chest.*

**taker** *n.* one who accepts an offer; a buyer. ♦ *Are there any takers for this fine, almost new caddy?*

**talk like a nut** *in.* to say stupid things. ♦ *You're talking like a nut! You don't know what you are saying.*

**talk on the big white phone** *in.* to vomit into a toilet. ♦ *One more beer and I'm gonna have to go talk on the big white phone.*

**talking head** *n.* a television news reader or announcer whose head and neck appear on the screen. ♦ *I've had it with talking heads. I can read the paper and learn as much in twenty minutes.*

**tall timbers** *n.* some remote well-forested place; the boonies. ♦ *Oh, Chuck lives out in the tall timbers somewhere. He only has a post office box number.*

**tallywhacker** *n.* the penis. ♦ *Stop scratching your tallywhacker in public!*

**tamp** *n.* a tampon. ♦ *You need a tamp, honey?*

**tanker** *n.* a drinker; a drunkard. ♦ *When I came into the bar, a few tankers were in the back.*

**tanky** *mod.* alcohol intoxicated. ♦ *He found a way to slow down and keep from getting tanky at parties.*

**tanned** *mod.* alcohol intoxicated. (Preserved like a tanned hide of an animal.) ♦ *Tom is too tanned to drive. Get him out of that car.*

**tap out 1.** *in.* to lose one's money gambling or in the securities markets. ♦ *I'm gonna tap out in about three more rolls—just watch.* ♦ *I really tapped out on that goldmining stock.* **2.** *in.* to die; to expire. ♦ *Mary was so tired that she thought she was going to tap out.*

**taped** [tept] *mod.* finalized; sealed (up); cinched. (As if one were taping a package.) ♦ *I'll have this deal taped by Thursday. Then we can take it easy.*

**tard** *n.* a person who behaves as if retarded. (Derogatory and potentially cruel.) ♦ *You tard! Why did you do that?*

**tat** *n.* a tattoo. ♦ *Nice tats!*

**tawny** ['tɔni] *mod.* excellent. ♦ *Who is throwing this tawny party anyway?*

**team Xerox** *n.* the imaginary source of copied documents, such as term papers. (Implies cheating or plagiarism. *Xerox* is a protected trade name.) ♦ *I got the term paper in on time with the help of team Xerox.*

**tear** SO **a new asshole** AND **tear** SO **a new one** to chastise someone severely. (Usually objectionable.) ♦ *The colonel glared at him and threatened to tear him a new asshole.* ♦ *If you don't get it right this time, I'll tear you a new one!*

**tech-nerd** ['tɛknɚd] *n.* a technically oriented, dull person, typically a male computer enthusiast. ♦ *My brother, who is a tech-nerd, spends more than ten hours a day on his computer.*

**telly** ['tɛli] *n.* a television set. (Originally British.) ♦ *What's on the telly tonight?*

**temp-tat** *n.* a temporary tattoo. (Viewed as wimpy by those bearing real ink.) ♦ *My father nearly croaked until I convinced him they were temp-tats.*

a **ten** *n.* the highest rank on a scale of one to ten. ♦ *On a scale of one to ten, this pizza's a ten.*

**that way 1.** *mod.* in love. ♦ *Well, Martha's that way, but Sam's just out for a good time.* **2.** *mod.* alcohol intoxicated. ♦ *I'm sorry, but Fred's that way again and can't drive to work.* **3.** *mod.* homosexual. ♦ *Ken said that you-know-who was acting sort of that way. What a gossip!*

**That's so suck!** *phr.* That's so awful. ♦ *Eat sweet potatoes? That's so suck!*

**That's the way the ball bounces.** *sent.* That is life.; That is the random way things happen. ♦ *It's tough, I know, but that's the way the ball bounces.*

**That's the way the cookie crumbles.** *sent.* That is life.; That is typical of the unequal share of things you are likely to get in life. ♦ *I lost my job. Oh, well. That's the way the cookie crumbles.*

**That's the way the mop flops.** *sent.* This is the way things happen.; This is typical of a random pattern of events. (Contrived.) ♦ *Sorry to hear about that, but that's the way the mop flops.*

**The Force** *n.* duct (duck) tape. ♦ *She used The Force to hold it all together.*

**There's nobody home.** *sent.* There are no brains in someone's head. ♦ *You twit! There's nobody home—that's for sure.*

**There you go. 1.** *sent.* Hooray! You did it right! (Usually **There you go!**) ♦ *Good shot, Chuck! There ya go!* **2.** *sent.* That is the way things are, just like I told you.; Isn't this just what you would expect? ♦ *There you go. Isn't that just like a man!* **3.** *sent.* You are doing it again. ♦ *I just told you not to put that junk on the table, and there you go.*

**think-piece** *n.* a thoughtful piece of writing in a newspaper or magazine. ♦ *Mr. Wilson's think-piece about the need for more concern for the middle class was not well received.*

**thou** [θaʊ] *n.* one thousand. ♦ *I managed to get a couple of thou from the bank, but I need a little more than that.*

**thrash on** *so in.* to scold, criticize, or berate someone. ♦ *She's always thrashing on her roommate.*

**threads** *n.* clothing. ♦ *When'd you get new threads, man?*

**throat** *n.* an earnest student; a *cutthroat* student. (Collegiate.) ♦ *Martin is not a throat! He's not that smart.*

**throg** *in.* to drink beer or liquor. (Possibly *throw* + *grog*.) ♦ *The guys were throgging till early beams.*

**throw a map** *tv.* to empty one's stomach; to vomit. ♦ *Somebody threw a map on the sidewalk.*

**throw down** *in.* to eat; to gobble one's food. (The opposite of *throw up* = to vomit.) ♦ *Man, I'm starved. Let's find a hamburger joint and throw down.*

**throw** one's **voice** *tv.* to empty one's stomach; to vomit. ♦ *Willy's in the john throwing his voice.*

**throw salt on** so's **game** *tv.* to mess up someone's plans. ♦ *I don't mean to throw salt on your game, but I don't think you can pull it off.*

**throw up** one's **toenails** *tv.* to wretch; to vomit a lot. ♦ *It sounded like he was throwing up his toenails.*

**thumber** ['θəmɚ] *n.* a beggar; a moocher. (As one who thumbs or begs a ride.) ♦ *Don't be a thumber, Frank. Go buy your own cancer sticks.*

**thunder-thighs** *n.* big or fat thighs. (Cruel. Also a rude term of address.) ♦ *Here, thunder-thighs, let me get you a chair or two.*

**tickle the ivories** *tv.* to play the piano. ♦ *I used to be able to tickle the ivories real nice.*

**tiffled** ['tɪfld] *mod.* alcohol intoxicated. ♦ *Harry was too tiffled to drive.*

**time to cruise** *n.* Time to leave. ♦ *Time to cruise. We're gone.*

**tin cow** *n.* canned milk. ♦ *This tin cow is okay in coffee or something, but you can't drink it.*

**tin dog** *n.* a snowmobile (in Alaska). ♦ *Who's out there riding the tin dog?*

**tin grin** *n.* a smile with a mouth having braces. ♦ *I'll be glad when I get rid of this tin grin.*

**tin hat** *n.* a soldier's helmet. ♦ *You use your tin hat for everything—washing, hauling water—you name it.*

**tingle 1.** *n.* a party. ♦ *This tingle is really da bomb.* **2.** *in.* to party. ♦ *Hey, man, let's tingle.*

**tinklebox** *n.* a piano. ♦ *The tinklebox in the bar seemed to be a bit loud.*

**tinsel-teeth** *n.* a nickname for someone who wears dental braces. (Also a rude nickname.) ♦ *Well, tinsel-teeth, today's the day your braces come off.*

**tints** *n.* sunglasses. ♦ *I have to get some prescription tints.*

**titless wonder 1.** *n.* an oafish or awkward person. (Usually objectionable.) ♦ *That stupid jerk is the classic titless wonder. What a twit!* **2.** *n.* an unsatisfactory thing or situation. ♦ *I've got to take this titless wonder into the shop for an oil change.*

**tits up** *mod.* upside down; on its or someone's back. (Usually objectionable.) ♦ *Her lousy pie fell tits up onto the kitchen floor.*

**to boot** *mod.* in addition. ♦ *She got an F on her term paper and flunked the final to boot.*

**toe jam** *n.* a nasty, smelly substance that collects between the toes of unwashed feet. ♦ *Wash your feet, you turkey! I don't want you getting all your toe jam all over the room!*

**toe tag** *tv.* to kill someone. (Bodies in the morgue are identified by tags on their big toes.) ♦ *Man, you treat me that way one more time and I'm gonna toe tag you!*

**tokus** AND **tukkis; tuchus** ['tokəs AND 'tʊkəs] *n.* the buttocks; the rump. (Yiddish.) ♦ *Look at the tukkis on that fat guy.*

**tonic** *n.* liquor. ♦ *Just a bit of tonic. I'm cutting down.*

**tootle along** *in.* to depart. ♦ *I think I'd better tootle along now.*

**tootonium** ['tu'toniəm] *n.* an imaginary, potent type of cocaine. (Drugs. A play on *titanium*.) ♦ *He called it tootonium. She called it trouble.*

**top story** AND **upper story** *n.* the brain. ♦ *I don't think her top story is occupied.* ♦ *A little weak in the upper story, but other than that, a great guy.*

**top-drawer** *mod.* top-quality. ♦ *I want to hire a young MBA who's top-drawer.*

**tornado juice** *n.* whiskey; strong whiskey. ♦ *This "tornado juice" smells like antifreeze.*

**torqued** [torkt] **1.** *mod.* angry; bent. ♦ *Now, now! Don't get torqued!* **2.** *mod.* drunk. (A play on **twisted**.) ♦ *Mary gets torqued on just a few drinks.*

**totalled 1.** *mod.* wrecked; damaged beyond repair. (From totally wrecked.) ♦ *The car was totaled. There was nothing that could be saved.* **2.** *mod.* alcohol intoxicated. ♦ *Tom was too totalled to talk.*

**totally** *mod.* absolutely; completely. (Standard. Achieves slang status through overuse.) ♦ *How totally gross!*

**totally awesome** *mod.* very, very impressive. ♦ *His motorcycle is totally awesome. It must have cost a fortune.*

**totally clueless** *mod.* ignorant (of something). ♦ *Everybody was totally clueless as to what to do.*

**touchy-feely** *mod.* very sensitive and empathetic; pretentiously compassionate. ♦ *Marge is so touchy-feely. She worries that anything she says may possibly offend someone.*

**touron** *n.* tourist moron. ♦ *Another touron tried to take a bath in a hot spring this morning.*

**toxic waste dump** *n.* a horrible person or place. ♦ *Frank, stop acting like a toxic waste dump and do as you're asked.*

**toxicated** AND **toxy** ['tɑksəkedəd AND 'tɑksi] *mod.* alcohol intoxicated. ♦ *The boss showed up totally toxicated after lunch and shocked the secretaries.*

**trad** [træd] *mod.* traditional. ♦ *A more trad style might make the grownups more comfortable.*

**traf** [træf] *n.* a release of intestinal gas. (This is **fart** spelled backward. Usually objectionable.) ♦ *Who let the traf?*

**trailer park trash** AND **TPT** *n.* trailer park trash. ♦ *My motor home cost more than your house, and you call me TPT?*

**trailer trash** *n.* the poorest of people who live in run-down house trailers in bad neighborhoods. (Used with singular or plural force. Rude and derogatory.) ♦ *She's just trailer trash. Probably doesn't even own shoes.*

**tranny** ['træni] **1.** *n.* an automobile transmission. ♦ *It looks like you get a new tranny, and I get 900 bucks.* **2.** *n.* a transgendered person. ♦ *She said she was a tranny, but nobody could tell.*

**trans** [trænts] *n.* an automobile. (From *transportation*.) ♦ *I don't have any trans—I can't get myself anywhere.* ♦ *What are you using for trans these days?*

**traps** *n.* the trapezium muscles, considered in pairs. (Bodybuilding.) ♦ *This exercise is really good for your traps.*

**Trash it!** *tv.* Throw it away! ♦ *We don't have space for this old chair. Trash it!*

**tree-suit** *n.* a wooden coffin. ♦ *You'd better shut up if you don't want to end up wearing a tree-suit.*

**tribe** *n.* a group of friends or relatives. ♦ *When are you and your tribe going to come for a visit?*

**tripe 1.** *n.* nonsense. ♦ *That's just tripe. Pay no attention.*
**2.** *n.* a bad performance; something worthless. ♦ *I know tripe when I see tripe, and that was tripe.*

**tris** [traɪz] *n.* the triceps. ♦ *I'm working on building up my tris. Been doing lots of pushups.*

**trojan horse** *n.* a kind of malicious software that arrives at a personal computer embedded in some other software and then introduces routines that can gather personal information or destroy the operationality of the computer. ♦ *The consultant called the intruder a "trojan horse" and said I needed yet another program to get rid of it.*

**troll booth** *n.* a (highway) toll booth. ♦ *There's another troll booth up ahead!*

**trouser snake** AND **trouser trout** *n.* the penis. ♦ *The doctor was taken aback when young Willard used the term "trouser snake." ♦ Stop scratching your trouser trout in public.*

**Truth, justice, and the American Way** AND **TJATAW** *phr. & comp. abb.* a phrase said in response to impassioned declarations about almost anything. (This phrase was used to introduce the *Superman* radio and television programs.) ♦ *Sure, Mom and apple pie, as well as TJATAW.*

**(T)sup?** [ˈ(t)səp] *interrog.* What's up?; What is happening?; What have you been doing? ♦ *Hi! Tsup?*

**tude** [tud] *n.* a bad *attitude.* ♦ *Hey, you really got a tude, dude.*

**tunage** [ˈtunɪdʒ] *n.* music; tunes. ♦ *My stereo is down and I'm running a tunage deficit.*

**tune out** *in.* to begin to ignore everything. ♦ *The entire class had tuned out, so no one heard the teacher ask the question.*

**tunes** *n.* a record; a record album; music in general. ♦ *I got some new tunes. Wanna come over and listen?*

**turd face** *n.* a wretched and obnoxious person. (Rude and derogatory.) ♦ *You stupid turd face! Why did you do that?*

**turkey bacon** *n.* a (untrained) night watchman; a uniformed but unoffical "police officer;" fake **bacon** = cop. ♦ *The place is guarded by creeky-kneed turkey bacon. I'll distract them while you sneak in.*

**turn on the waterworks** *in.* to begin to cry. ♦ *His lower lip was quivering, and I knew he was going to turn on the waterworks.*

**turn one's toes up** *tv.* to die. ♦ *The cat turned up its toes right after church. Ah, the power of prayer.*

**turn turtle** *in.* to turn over, as with a ship. ♦ *The old dog finally turned turtle, and that was the end.*

**turtle heading** *n.* popping up and down in an office cubicle, looking at what's going on in the rest of the office. (See also **prairie dog**.) ♦ *Everybody was turtle heading, trying to see what was happening in Willy's cubicle.*

**tush(y)** *n.* the buttocks. (Probably from Yiddish.) ♦ *I fell down right on my tush.*

**twack** *n.* a twelve pack of beer (cans). (Twelve + pack.) ♦ *Let's pick up a couple of twacks for the game.*

**tweak** [tʍik] *tv.* to adjust something slightly. ♦ *Tweak the tuner a little and see if you can get that station just a little bit clearer.*

**twenty-twenty hindsight** AND **20/20 hindsight** *n.* an ability to figure out what one should have done after it is too late to do it. ♦ *Everybody has twenty-twenty hindsight!*

**two-bit** *mod.* cheap; small-time. ♦ *Max is just a two-bit pusher. I want Mr. Big.*

**twofer** ['tufɚ] *n.* an item that is selling two for the price of one. ♦ *Here's a good deal—a twofer—only $7.98.* ♦ *Everything in this store is a twofer. I only want one of these. Do I have to bring a friend who wants one, too?*

**two-planker** *n.* a skier. (From a snowboarder's point of view.) ♦ *A couple of two-plankers zoomed past us and scared us to death.*

**two-topper** *n.* a restaurant table that will seat two people. (Restaurant jargon.) ♦ *There are two-toppers on each side of the kitchen door.*

# U

**Uncle nab** *n.* a policeman. ♦ *Watch out for Uncle nab. He's been asking about you.*

**uncool** *mod.* square; dull and orthodox. ♦ *This place is uncool. Let's cruise.*

**underpinnings** *n.* the legs. ♦ *He has good underpinnings—ought to be able to run faster.* ♦ *With underpinnings like that, he ought to be able to win the marathon.*

**underwhelm** *tv. & in.* to fail to impress (someone). ♦ *As we were being underwhelmed by a buxom soprano, my thoughts drifted to more pleasant matters.*

**unlax** [ən'læks] *in.* to unwind and relax. ♦ *I just can't wait to get home and unlax.*

**unobtanium** *n.* something highly desirable that cannot be found; a fantastic, perfect metallic substance. (See also **obtanium**.) ♦ *Of course, his bike is made of unobtanium and should stand up in a volcanic eruption.*

**up close and personal** *phr.* intimately; more intimately than one might have wished for. (Colloq. The phrase has been the title of a movie and the name of a television show.) ♦ *When my trunks slipped down, she got to know me a little more up close and personal that we were ready for at that moment.*

**up in** so's **gold ones** AND **up on** so's **bumper.** *n.* in someone's face. (Alludes to gold teeth.) ♦ *He had his smelly face up in my gold ones, so I clobbered him.* ♦ *Why are you up on my bumper, dawg?*

**up the pole** *mod.* alcohol intoxicated. ♦ *You sound a little up the pole. Why don't you call back when you're sober?*

**up time** *n.* the time when a computer is running. ♦ *On some systems the down time is longer than the up time.*

**up to** one's **eyeballs** AND **up to** one's **ears** *mod.* filled up with something. ♦ *We are up to our eyeballs with trouble around here.* ♦ *She's up to her ears in marriage proposals.*

**uppity** ['əpədi] *mod.* haughty. (Folksy.) ♦ *Why is she so uppity?*

the **urge to purge** *n.* the need to throw up. ♦ *Pete felt the urge to purge and ran for the john.*

**UVs** ['ju'viz] *n.* ultraviolet rays from the sun; sunshine. (Initialism.) ♦ *I wanna get some UVs before we go home.*

# V

**vacation** *n.* a prison sentence. (Underworld.) ♦ *It was a three-year vacation, with time off for good behavior.*

**vanilla 1.** *mod.* plain; dull. (See also beige.) ♦ *The entire production was sort of vanilla, but it was okay.* **2.** *n.* a Caucasian. ♦ *Some vanilla's on the phone—selling something, I guess.*

**veggy** AND **veggie** ['vedʒi] **1.** *n.* a vegetarian. ♦ *We have a lovely salad bar for the veggies among you.* **2.** *n.* a vegetable; a chunk or piece of vegetable. (Usually plural.) ♦ *Do you want any veggies with this?* **3.** *n.* a comatose patient in a hospital. (Medical.) ♦ *Mary's aunt has been a veggie in the hospital for more than a year.* **4.** *n.* someone who is tired or exhausted. ♦ *I want to be a veggy this weekend. I'll just stay at home and relax.*

**vertical bathtub** *n.* a men's urinal. ♦ *When I walked into the room with vertical bathtubs, I knew I was in the wrong place.*

**vibes** [vaɪbz] *n.* vibrations; atmosphere; feelings. (Usually with *good* or *bad*.) ♦ *I just don't get good vibes about this deal.*

**vic** [vɪk] **1.** *n.* a victim. (Streets. See also vivor.) ♦ *We're all vics, but we all keep going.* **2.** *n.* a convict. ♦ *We try*

225

*to give the vics a chance at employment where they won't be treated badly.*

**vicious** ['vɪʃəs] *mod.* great; excellent. ♦ *Man, this burger is really vicious.*

**vicked** [vɪkt] *mod.* cheated; victimized. (See also **vic**.) ♦ *I feel so vicked when I see where my taxes are spent.*

**vines** *n.* clothing. (Black.) ♦ *Good-looking vines on that guy, right?*

**vivor** ['vɑɪvɚ] *n.* a survivor; a street person who manages to survive. (Streets. Compare this with **vic**.) ♦ *Harry's a vivor, and I like him.*

**viz** [vɑɪz] *n.* Levis; blue jeans. ♦ *Those viz are too tight for her.*

**vújà day** *mod.* describes the feeling of never having been in a place before or having never had the current experience before. (A play on *déjà vu*.) ♦ *I was lost! I looked around, and a feeling of vújà day crept over me!*

# W

**wailing** AND **whaling** *mod.* excellent. (Teens.) ♦ *What a whaling guitar!*

**walk heavy** *in.* to be important. (Black.) ♦ *Harry's been walking heavy since he graduated.*

**walk on sunshine** *n.* to be really happy. ♦ *I'm in love and I'm walking on sunshine.*

**walking wounded 1.** *n.* soldiers who are injured but still able to walk. (Standard English.) ♦ *Many of the walking wounded helped with the more seriously injured cases.* **2.** *n.* a person who is injured—mentally or physically—and still able to go about daily life. ♦ *The outpatient clinic was filled with the walking wounded.* **3.** *n.* stupid people in general. ♦ *Most of network programming seems to be aimed at the walking wounded of our society.*

**walkover** *n.* an easy victory; an easy task. (From sports.) ♦ *Learning the computer's operating system was no walkover for me.*

**wall job** *n.* a car—in the shop for repairs—which is parked against the wall with no repairs done. (The customer is charged anyway.) ♦ *Places like those we surveyed may charge hundreds of dollars for what they call "wall jobs."*

**Walla!** AND **Wala!; Wallah!; Viola!** [wɑ 'lɑ] ♦ *exclam.* And there you have it! (All versions are misspellings or misunderstandings of the French *Voila!* The *Viola!* is a well-meant spelling error.) ♦ *And walla! There it is. Cooked just right!*

**wallet** *n.* a college student's parents and financial source. ♦ *My wallet won't send me another penny this semester.*

**wampum** ['wɑmpəm] *n.* money. (From an American Indian word.) ♦ *I don't have enough wampum to swing the deal.*

**wana** ['wɑnə] *n.* marijuana. (Drugs.) ♦ *How much is this wana, man?*

**wand waver** AND **wagger** an exhibitionist. ♦ *The cops picked up a wand waver on Main Street.*

**war paint** *n.* a woman's makeup. ♦ *She'll be ready when she gets on her war paint.*

**warchalking** *n.* making a mark in a location where a wireless interconnection is available. ♦ *Since more and more Wi-Fi hot spots are available, warchalking has become rare.*

**wardrobing** *n.* the practice of buying clothing, wearing it once, and returning it for a refund. ♦ *The company put a stop to wardrobing by making customers mail their returns to a central warehouse.*

**washboard abs** *n.* heavily marked abdominal muscles, divided into six equal sections. ♦ *If I work out hard enough I can build those washboard abs.*

**waspish** *mod.* in the manner of a WASP (White Anglo-Saxon Protestant). ♦ *She looks sort of "waspish," but she's not.*

**water** one's **cheeks** *tv.* to cry; to shed tears sobbing. ♦ *Poor Billy was watering his cheeks all night because his dog ran away.*

**weblog** AND **blog** *n.* a type of online diary that someone makes available to other people on the Internet. (A very popular way to communicate one's personal details without any social interaction.) ♦ *John started a weblog so that other people could read about what he eats for breakfast.* ♦ *I deleted my blog since it was too silly.*

**weeper** *n.* a sad movie, novel, television program, etc. ♦ *I can't seem to get enough of these weepers.*

**wet one** *n.* a cold beer. ♦ *I could sure use a wet one about now.*

**wet sock** AND **wet rag** *n.* a wimp; a useless jerk. (See also rubber sock.) ♦ *Don't be such a wet sock! Stand up for your rights!* ♦ *Willard is a wet rag, but he's kind and helpful.*

**wetware** ['wetwer] *n.* the human brain. (Compared to computer *hardware* and *software*.) ♦ *This isn't a hardware problem; it's a wetware problem.*

**whankster** AND **wankster; whangster; wangster** *n.* a phony gangsta; a bogus, nonblack, ghetto dweller, affecting the language and dress of the streets. (The "w" and "wh" difference is dialectal. Derived from *white* + *gangster*, although some say *white* + *whanker* = masturbator.) ♦ *He's a phony and a whankster!*

**What's going down?** *interrog.* What's happening? ♦ *Hey, man, what's going down?*

**What's happ(ening)?** *interrog.* Hello, what's new? ♦ *Hey, dude! What's happening?*

**What's really good witcha?** *interrog.* How are you? ♦ *Mooshoo! What's really good witcha?*

**What's the dilly?** *interrog.* What's going on?; What's the deal? (*Dilly* is a pronunciation of *dealy*.) ♦ *Who's shouting? What's the dilly?*

**What's the (good) word?** *interrog.* Hello, how are you? ♦ *Haven't seen you in a long time. What's the good word?*

**What's the scam?** AND **What's the deal?** *interrog.* What is going on around here?; Explain what is happening or what you are doing. ♦ *What's the scam? What's happening, dude?* ♦ *I gave you a twenty, and you give me five back? What's the deal? Where's my other five?*

**What's up?** *interrog.* What is going on?; What is happening? (See also (T)sup?; Wusup?) ♦ *Haven't seen you in a month of Sundays. What's up?*

**What's your damage?** *interrog.* What's your problem? (Like a *damage* report.) ♦ *You look beat, man. What's your damage?*

**where** SO **is at** *in.* what mental condition someone is in. ♦ *You said it! I know just where you're at!*

**where** SO **lives** *in.* at one's core; in one's own personal situation. ♦ *That really hits you where you live, doesn't it?*

**where** so's **head is at** *in.* the state of one's mental well-being. ♦ *As soon as I figure where my head is at, I'll be okay.*

**whiffled** ['mɪf[l]d] *mod.* alcohol intoxicated. ♦ *Jed found himself a mite whiffled, but nobody else knew.*

**whigga** AND **wigga; whigger; wigger** *n.* a gangsta term for a nonblack who affects the speech, dress, and behavior of the black males of ghetto or streets. (Streets. Derogatory. A blend of *white* + *nigga*.) ♦ *Not bad for a whigga.*

**white knuckler 1.** *n.* a tense and nervous person. ♦ *You white knucklers are just going to have to relax.* **2.** *n.* a suspenseful event, such as an exciting movie or a rough airplane flight. ♦ *The movie was a real white knuckler.*

**white man's disease** *n.* the inability to jump in basketball. ♦ *You break your leg, Walter? Or you got a case of white man's disease?*

**whitebread** *mod.* plain; dull. ♦ *If I wanted a white bread vacation, I'd have gone to the beach.*

**Who's your daddy?** *interrog.* Who is your boss? It's me isn't it? (A reminder of who's the boss.) ♦ *Don't waver. Do it! Who's your daddy?*

the **whole schmear** [...ʃmɪr] *n.* the entire amount; the entire affair. (Based on Yiddish.) ♦ *I'll take a hamburger with everything on it—the whole schmear.*

the **whole shebang** AND the **whole shooting match** [...ʃə'bæŋ] *n.* the whole affair; everything and everyone. (Folksy.) ♦ *The whole shebang is just about washed up.* ♦ *The boss put an end to the whole shooting match.*

**whoopie cakes** *n.* female buttocks. ♦ *You put those whoopie cakes back down in that chair and listen to me!*

**Whuhap?** *interrog.* Hello.; What's new? (Black. A greeting inquiry.) ♦ *Whuhap? Where's the action?*

**wicked** *mod.* excellent; impressive; cool. (Also in compounds, *wicked smart, wicked cool, etc.*) ♦ *Now this is what I call a wicked guitar.*

**wicked bad** *mod.* really quite good. (*Bad* has a long history of being used as an intensifier. *Wicked* here is a synonym of the intensifier *bad.*) ♦ *Man, this stuff is wicked bad.*

**wicky** *mod.* wicked; excellent. ♦ *Whose wicky red convertible is parked in front of the house?*

**wiener nose** ['winɚ...] *n.* a simpleton. (Also a derogatory term of address.) ♦ *Look, wiener nose, mind your own business.*

**Wilma** ['wɪlmə] *n.* a stupid woman. (From the Flintstones character. Also a term of address.) ♦ *She is such a Wilma! What a twit!*

**wino** ['waɪno] **1.** *n.* wine. ♦ *How about a little more wino?* **2.** *n.* a wine drunkard. ♦ *I gave the wino some money to help him stop the shakes.*

**with it** *mod.* up-to-date; contemporary. ♦ *Come on, chum. Get with it.*

**within spitting distance** *mod.* close by. ♦ *The house you're looking for is within spitting distance, but it's hard to find.*

**wombat** ['wɑmbæt] *n.* a strange person; a geek. (Collegiate.) ♦ *Who's the wombat in the 1957 Chevy?*

**wonder water** *n.* steroids. ♦ *Look at the guns on that dude! Must be using wonder water.*

**wonk** [woŋk] **1.** *n.* an earnest student. (Collegiate.) ♦ *Yes, you could call Martin a wonk. In fact, he's the classic wonk.* **2.** *n.* a bureaucrat; a flunky. ♦ *The State Department policy wonks were up all night putting together the report.*

**wonky** ['woŋki] *mod.* studious. (Collegiate.) ♦ *You ought to get a little wonky yourself.*

**woody 1.** *n.* a wooden surfboard; a surfboard. ♦ *Get your woody, and let's get moving.* **2.** *n.* an erection of the penis. ♦ *His morning woody made a little mountain with the sheets on his bed.*

**word of mouse** *n.* a message spread by e-mail. (Contrived. Refers to a computer mouse. A play on *word of mouth*.) ♦ *A lot of these jokes are spread by word of mouse.*

the **works** *n.* the entire amount; everything. ♦ *I'd like my hamburger with onions, pickles, ketchup, mustard—the works.* ♦ *She's getting the works at the beauty shop—cut, wash, dye, and set.*

**worm** *n.* a repellent person, usually a male. ♦ *Gad, you are a worm, Tom.*

**worm burner** *n.* a fast, but low-rolling ball in golf, baseball, etc. ♦ *Walter sent a worm burner down the third-base line.*

**worm-food** *n.* a corpse. ♦ *You wanna end up worm-food? Just keep smarting off.*

**worms in blood** *n.* spaghetti in tomato sauce. ♦ *I'm getting tired of worms in blood every Wednesday.*

**would not be seen dead** *phr.* would not do something under any circumstances. ♦ *I wouldn't be seen dead going out with Spike!*

**wrench** *n.* a mechanic. (Possibly from *Mr. Goodwrench.*) ♦ *I gotta get my ride in and have a wrench look at the serpentine.*

**wrinkle-rod** *n.* the crankshaft of an engine. ♦ *A wrinkle-rod'll set you back about $199, plus installation charges, of course.*

**wrong side of the tracks** *n.* the poor side of town. ♦ *I'm glad I'm from the wrong side of the tracks. I know what life is really like.*

**wuffo** *n.* an (imaginary) annoying person who keeps asking why = what for = **wuffo.** ♦ *I was trying to get here on time, but a wuffo was holding me hostage.*

**Wusup?** AND **Wassup?** *interrog.* What's up? ♦ *Hey, man! Wassup?*

**X'd out 1.** *mod.* eliminated; crossed-out. ♦ *But the Babbits are X'd out.* **2.** *mod.* killed. (Underworld.) ♦ *Mr. Big wanted Pete X'd out.*

**XMT** *tv.* excuse my typing; I am sorry I type so poorly. (Used in e-mail and computer forum or newsgroup messages. Not pronounced aloud.) ♦ *XMT. I have a sore finger and I keep hitting the wrong keys.*

**XYZ** *tv.* examine your zipper; make sure your fly is zipped up. (Initialism. Said to men when necessary.) ♦ *I say there, Willy, XYZ.*

# Y

**yada, yada, yada** AND **Y3** *phr. & comp. abb.* talk, talk, talk. ♦ *Y3. What utter B.S.*

**yank** SO's **crank** *tv.* to tease a male sexually. ♦ *Don't pay any attention to her. She's just yanking your crank.*

**yard** *n.* a one-hundred-dollar bill. (Underworld.) ♦ *The guy wanted a yard just to fix a little dent in the fender.*

**yard-sale** *n.* the site of a crash involving one or more bikes, skateboards, snowboards, etc., where the debris is spread far and wide. (Looking like a disorganized yard-, garage-, or tag-sale. ♦ *Man, did you see that yard-sale at the last turn?*

**Yello.** ['jɛ'lo] *interj.* Hello. (Said with any intonation that would be appropriate with *hello*.) ♦ *Yello, Smith residence.*

**yench** [jɛntʃ] *tv.* to swindle someone; to victimize someone. (Underworld.) ♦ *The flimflam artist yenched a couple of banks and then moved on.*

**yenta** ['jɛntə] *n.* a gossip, usually a woman. (Regarded as Yiddish.) ♦ *She can be such a yenta when she's got news.*

**yo mama** *interj.* so you say. (Black.) ♦ *Not enough bread! Yo mama.*

**yoink** sth *tv.* to steal something. ♦ *He yoinked a bike from the rack.*

**yoked** [jokt] *mod.* having well-marked abdominal muscles; have heavy muscles. ♦ *That guy is really yoked. I wonder how much he works out.*

**yokes** *n.* muscles; abdominal muscles. (See also yoked. Also seen as *yolks.* Possibly as if muscular shoulders can be seen as yokes of muscle.) ♦ *Look at the yokes on that broad.*

**yolk** *n.* semen. (Possibly confused with egg white.) ♦ *Clean up that yolk before somebody sees it.*

**You can't dance at two weddings.** *sent.* You cannot do two things at once. ♦ *Either go to the beach with Fred or stay here with me. You can't dance at two weddings.*

**You guys bitchin'?** *interrog.* Hello, how are you? ♦ *Tsup? You guys bitchin'?*

**(You) want a piece of me?** *interrog.* Do you want to fight with me? ♦ *Come on, Wussy. You want a piece of me?*

**You want to step outside?** *interrog.* Do you intend to start a fight?; Shall we go outside and fight? ♦ *You want to step outside? We can settle this once and for all.*

**Your mileage may vary.** and **YMMV** *sent. & comp. abb.* You may have a different experience or different results. ♦ *It worked for me. Your mileage may vary.*

**yutz** [juts] *n.* a fool; a simpleton. ♦ *Don't act like such a yutz!*

# Z

**zarf** [zɑrf] *n.* an ugly and repellent male. ♦ *That zarf is Martin, and he makes all As, and he helps me with my homework, so just shut up!*

**zebra** *n.* a referee. (Because of the black-and-white striped shirt.) ♦ *The zebra blew the whistle on almost every play.*

**zeek out** [zik...] *in.* to lose control of oneself. ♦ *I was in a pretty bad state. I almost zeeked out.*

**zerk** [zɚk] *n.* a stupid person; a jerk. ♦ *Don't be a zerk! Do what you're told.*

**zhlubby** ['ʒləbi] *mod.* dull; boorish. (See also **schlub**.) ♦ *I can't sit through this zhlubby thing one more minute.*

**zilch** [zɪltʃ] *n.* nothing. ♦ *And what do I get? Zilch, that's what!*

**zipper morals** *n.* loose morals that lead to the easy unzipping of clothing. ♦ *Ah, youth and its zipper morals!*

**zit** [zɪt] *n.* a pimple. ♦ *Don't squeeze your zits on my mirror!*

**zob** [zɑb] *n.* a worthless person; a nobody. ♦ *Another zob came in to try out for the part.*

**zonk** [zɔŋk] **1.** *tv.* to overpower someone or something. ♦ *We zonked the dog with a kick.* **2.** *tv.* to tire someone out. (See also **zonk out**.) ♦ *The pills zonked me, but they made my cold better.*

**zonk out** *in.* to collapse from exhaustion; to go into a stupor from drugs or exhaustion; to go to sleep. ♦ *I'm gonna go home and zonk out.*

**zoobang** ['zubæŋ] *mod.* alcohol intoxicated. ♦ *Boy howdy! Are you ever zoobang!*

**zooted** ['zudəd] *mod.* alcohol intoxicated. ♦ *Both of them were zooted to the max.*

**zosted** *mod.* drunk. (Like **toasted**.) ♦ *He's so zosted! He can't drive!*

**zotz** [zɑts] **1.** AND **zot**. [zɑt] *n.* zero; nothing. ♦ *I went out to get the mail, but there was zot.* **2.** *tv.* to kill someone or something. ♦ *Sam threatened to zotz Joel Cairo, but it was just a threat.*